Visual Journaling

Visual Journaling

Going Deeper than Words

BARBARA GANIM

&

SUSAN FOX

A publication supported by
THE KERN FOUNDATION

Quest Books
Theosophical Publishing House

Wheaton, Illinois ♦ Chennai (Madras), India

DEDICATION

To all the visual journalers who contributed their stories and imparted their wisdom so willingly.

First Quest Edition 1999

The Theosophical Publishing House
P.O. Box 270
Wheaton, IL 60189-0270

A publication of the Theosophical Publishing House,
a department of the Theosophical Society in America

Cover and text design and typesetting by Beth Hansen-Winter

Library of Congress Cataloging-in-Publication Data

Ganim, Barbara.
    Visual journaling: going deeper than words / Barbara Ganim & Susan Fox.
    p.   cm.
    Includes bibliographical references.
    ISBN 0-8356-0777-1
    1. Art therapy.   2. Diaries—Therapeutic use.   3. Imagery (Psychology)—Therapeutic
    use.   4. Self-help techniques.   I. Fox, Susan.   II. Title.
RC489.A7G36   1999
615.8′5156—dc21   99-24444
                                       CIP

5 4 3   *   01 02 03 04 05

Printed in Hong Kong through Global Interprint, Santa Rosa, California

ACKNOWLEDGMENTS

This book could never have been written were it not for the support and contributions of many people who believed in its importance and helped to make it a reality. First, we thank all the visual journalers who have taken our workshops through the years—you have taught us so much about this wonderful process.

We also wish to acknowledge by name each individual who generously contributed artwork, personal stories, ideas, suggestions and wisdom: Cherie Aiello, Rob Blais, Robin Boyd, Kerri Brennan, Brenda Bullinger, Patricia Carbotti, Sheila Charron, Bre Churchill, Sabra Churchill, Meg Corrigan, Carrol Cutler, Sarah Davis, Donna DiGiuseppe, Joan Dwyer, Ellen Fitzgerald, Sonja Fisher, Jeannine Gendron, Pauline Goulet, Robin Grace, Birgitta Grimm, Sandi Gold, Linda Hughes-Rivers, Carol Issaco, Beth Jackson, Adele Karbowski, Kyung Kim, Antoinette Ledzian, Kathy Mack, Cheryl McKenna, Barbara McKerriker, Patricia Marx, Robert Morse, Sandi O'Brien, Carole Patterson, Cheryl Ryan, Mary Sargent Sanger, Claire Sartori-Stein, Margaret Sherrer, Kate Siekierski, Lisa Slattery, Ishmira Kathleen Thoma, Christina Vivona, Linda Hill-Wall and Alayne White. Without each of you, this book truly could not have been written.

We would also like to thank our agent, Julie Anna Hill. You are our guiding star, our angel of faith and hope.

We thank Liliana Costa for your first-cut editing help with the proposal and beginning chapters and, as always, your valuable feedback on the concept of the book in the early stages of its development. You are a valued friend, supporter and collaborator.

We extend our thanks and gratitude to Brenda Rosen, executive editor at Quest Books, for your enthusiasm about this book from start to finish and the thoughtful ideas and insights you contributed as the book evolved.

We thank Jane Lawrence for a superb editing job. You honored our voice and loved the message we had to deliver. It doesn't get any better than that.

We also wish to thank those people who worked hard to help us meet our tight deadlines: Gerald Walsh, photographer, East Greenwich Photo, East Greenwich, Rhode Island; Raoul and Janice Holzinger of Print World in North Kingstown, Rhode Island; and Marilyn Johnson and Stacy Steinman, our transcriptionists.

And of course, we both thank our friends and families who so patiently supported us through this project.

CONTENTS

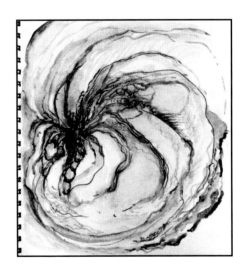

Taking the First Step

Visual Journaling as an Everyday Practice

Healing Your Stress-Producing Emotions

Conversing with Your Images

Art from the Heart

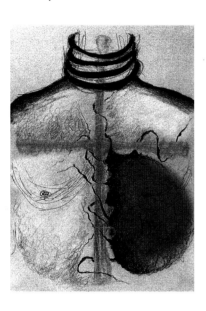

Special color section featuring selected pieces of artwork by visual journalers. The artwork is accompanied by a written statement reflecting the thoughts and heart-touching revelations each journaler had when they completed their piece. These journal images and the statements that accompany them are windows into the personal and very precious inner world of their creators. Only by sharing our inner-most thoughts and fears, as well as our deepest hopes and dreams, can we give others the courage to freely express what their hearts need to say.

Overcoming Fear

Resolving Inner Conflict Through Soul Wisdom

Expanding Your Visual-Journaling Experience

AUTHORS' NOTE

Because this book was written by two of us, it was difficult to separate our voices. Therefore we have consistently used the plural pronoun *we* throughout the text. However, there are occasional exceptions in which we found it necessary to identify ourselves individually, either because a particular section was relevant to one of our own individual experiences, or there was a specific reason to refer to the other by name.

We also want to advise you that the visual-journaling process can bring up emotional issues that you may not always be prepared to handle. If this occurs, we recommend that you see a professional counselor/therapist.

How Images Express What Words Cannot

Figure I-1. **Source of Power, of Rage,** *from the journal of Adele Karbowski*

We have discovered, through our work as expressive art therapists, that within all of us is a silent language that reveals the truth of our thoughts, feelings and emotions far more fluently than words. That language is imagery. Visual journaling is a process we developed to encourage our clients to express this inner language on a regular basis.

Visual journaling, like verbal journaling, is a way to record the nuances of life's experiences. But instead of words, visual journaling involves using one's inner vision to imagine what a thought, feeling or emotional reaction would look like if it were expressed as a color, shape or image. The act of drawing allows the journaler to see in graphic form what was initially an abstract, almost incomprehensible notion. Explaining in words how you feel when you lose a loved one or when you fall in love is for most of us an impossible task. Words simply can't describe such an experience. But images can—and with a depth that words cannot achieve.

Fascinated by the results our clients obtained when they drew images of how their emotional reactions felt inside their bodies, we began researching exactly how imagery is perceived by the body and mind. That's when we discovered the extensive work that had been done in the areas of sense perception, split-brain functioning and body-mind thought transmission. Our own recognition that imagery

1

Figure I-2. **Feeling Joy**, *from the journal of a workshop participant*

"When a feeling of joy comes over me, I sense a rainbow fountain of pure color beginning to flow from my heart into every cell of my body."

felt about experiences or issues in their lives, but as they began to understand this language, we also found that it communicated messages. These messages, it soon became apparent, were not from their rational, logical, conscious minds, but seemed to come from a deeper place—the realm of the subconscious mind, a source of wisdom we all possess but often ignore. It is a wisdom that sees beyond the rational mind's fragmented interpretation of life events into a deeper vision that reveals our inner truth and the purpose inherent in all our experiences. That wisdom, we believe, is *soul wisdom.*

is a language inherent in each individual was verified by our findings: imagery is the body-mind's first or primary means of inner communication. Words are a secondary form of outer communication—a method we have invented to communicate with each other. Our conviction that inner imagery is a more accurate way of expressing and understanding what we feel and think moved beyond mere speculation. We now had the research data to verify what our clients' experiences had shown us.

As we continued to work with our clients using visual journaling as their principal means of self-expression, we noticed that their imagistic language not only revealed the truth of how they

Before long, our clients began asking us to offer visual-journaling workshops where they could gather with others who were doing journal drawings, share the results and discuss what their inner imagery was teaching them. Consequently, over the last five years we have been conducting visual-journaling workshops for an ever growing number of participants. Most people who have come into these workshops have not yet left. They keep taking the workshop over and over again. They all tell us the same thing: without visual journaling, they would lose touch with who they are on the inside, that connection to their souls—a connection that keeps them walking their rightful path.

Figure I-3. Even stick figures and broad, undefined gestures or scribbles can beautifully and completely express the imagery of the soul.

During the years that we have been offering these workshops, we have solidified the process of learning how to keep a visual journal into a six-week program. Along with learning how to access and express emotions and feelings through imagery, our students are also introduced to the research documentation that substantiates and explains why this process works so well.

In this book we have taken all the components of our six-week workshop and put them together into an easy-to-follow format. If you commit to doing the exercises in this book, you too will learn how to access your inner language of imagery and express it through journal drawings. You will also, if you take the time to answer the self-exploration questions at the end of each exercise, learn how to understand this language. The self-exploration questions are designed to help you identify the images in your journal renderings as metaphoric and symbolic representations of your experiences, feelings, emotions, desires and expectations.

DEALING WITH FEAR AND SELF-DOUBT

If you are intrigued by the idea of keeping a visual journal, but feel a nagging sense of fear and self-doubt that you know nothing about drawing or art materials, you are not alone. Many of the people who have taken our workshops have voiced the same concerns. As we thought about the comments and questions that keep reemerging from the people in our groups, we decided that it might be helpful to share with you their thoughts and trepidations about the process. Here is what some of our workshop participants had to say when they first came into a group.

- I always wanted to try painting or drawing, but I didn't know how to use art materials.
- I will never be able to draw anything well!
- I had a bad experience with art in school; my art teacher told me to give it up because I had no talent.
- I'll never be able to do visual journaling because all I can draw are stick figures.
- I worry about what my drawings are going to look like. I'm afraid they will look childish.
- When I watch others jump right in and start drawing, I freeze up because I'm afraid my art won't look like theirs.
- I don't even know what I'm doing here because I can't draw. Every time I try it, I feel stupid. But for some reason, a little voice inside me keeps saying, "This time will be different."

Our response to all of these apprehensive remarks is: This time it *will* be different! You will find, just as each of these workshop participants did, that it doesn't matter if you don't know how to use art materials or if your drawings look like a five-year-old did them. If you can pick up a crayon or a piece of pastel chalk and make a simple mark on paper, we will show you how to look at that mark and understand what it's trying to tell you. You are about to learn how to communicate with the inner you through a language of color, shape and form that is surprisingly easy to comprehend. The meaning behind a stick figure or a swirling line will be just as clear to you as the meaning behind a detailed, realistic drawing. In fact, as you will see, people who draw too well often have great difficulty understanding what their journal drawings are about—they get so caught up in technique that they lose the message their imagery is attempting to convey.

Figure I-4. **Fear and Intimidation,** *from the journal of Ellen Fitzgerald*

YOU DON'T HAVE TO BE AN ARTIST

One of the best things about the visual-journaling process is that you don't have to be an artist, nor do you need any previous art experience or what some people call "artistic talent."

Everyone has the ability to express feelings and emotions using their inner language of imagery. Participants in our visual-journaling workshops have been surprised to discover just how easy it is to render their visualized imagery once they learn how to get past what they think their drawings should look like. It helps to remember that visual journaling is not about creating art, it is about expressing an imagistic language whose alphabet is color, shape, line, form and texture. The more simple and natural the rendering of this language, the more truthful the meaning. Even stick figures and broad, undefined gestures or scribbles can beautifully and completely express the imagery of the soul. When we work with people who are skilled artists, we often ask them to render their images with their nondominant hand to keep them from becoming too attached to the look of their imagery.

When Ellen Fitzgerald joined one of our visual-journaling workshops, she, like many new participants, felt so uncomfortable about her ability to draw that she was hesitant to share her first journal drawing (Figure I-4) with the group. With a little encouragement, she opened her journal and read what she had written above her drawing. "I feel intimidated by the concept of art. I feel like I can't make my hand do what my mind sees." Then she said, "When I was in high school, my art teacher told me that I shouldn't be in her class because I couldn't draw well enough. Ever since then I've been afraid to try." We asked her what made her want to take this workshop. She replied, "I've had this feeling for a long time that art could be a great way to express my emotions—if I could just get past my fear." By her second week in the workshop, Ellen was drawing her emotions with ease, confidence and a new sense of excitement. She had discovered that her way of drawing was more than good enough to express her inner language of imagery.

VISUAL JOURNALING HELPS YOU TO ACCESS YOUR INNER WISDOM

By using the visual-journaling process on a regular basis, you will be able to access the gentle guidance of your soul's wisdom. Through this inner wisdom, you will always know which choices and decisions are right for you with any issue you may be facing. This will help you avoid the inner conflict that so often occurs between thoughts and feelings that, as you will learn, is the fundamental cause of stress.

Anyone struggling with illness or disease will find that visual journaling is an excellent self-healing therapy, because stress, as research has shown, causes immune system dysfunction, cellular abnormality and the eventual degeneration of body systems. Visual journaling can help you to release stress and maintain your physical body in a state of healthy well-being.

Visual journaling can do more than just help you maintain a state of inner harmony, however. The *soul messages* you receive when you learn to understand your imagistic language will show you what changes need to occur in your life to begin healing from within.

USING VERBAL RESPONSES TO PROCESS A DRAWING

Although visual journaling is primarily focused on using imagery to express feelings and emotions, words are used to dialogue with yourself about your imagery. By combining verbal thoughts with imagistic perceptions, you will find that visual journaling serves as an important tool to integrate the functions of your visual, intuitive, feeling-centered right brain with your verbal, logical, thought-centered left brain. An image is an expansive way of perceiving an experience with all the subtleties that occur as the body-mind processes that experience. Words balance the process by contracting our perception, thus enabling us to discern and define the parameters of the experience. Our verbal responses to a drawing can actually help keep us focused once we have accessed an emotion or feeling through imagery.

While the main focus of this book is on how to do visual journaling, we also felt it was important to include examples of some of our workshop participants' journaling work, and in their own words to share with you what they have learned about themselves from their imagery. Our hope is that you will begin to understand through their experiences (as well as your own) the importance of reconnecting with your inner voice—the voice of your soul—and how visual journaling can be the key to accessing the divine, intuitive knowledge that unlocks the mysteries of your life.

Figure 1-1. **Fish,** *from the journal of Linda Hill-Wall*

"Visual journaling speaks a language deeper than words, drawing from within our beauty, our truth and our wisdom. It brings to paper the landscape of our life's serenities and struggles, joys and tears, passions, fears and dreams. It articulates our sacredness and our connectedness to all of creation."

CHAPTER ONE

Going Deeper than Words to Give Voice to Your Soul

Drawing is . . . above all a means of expressing intimate feelings and moods.

—Henri Matisse

Linda Hill-Wall was a longtime member of one of our ongoing visual-journaling workshops. The words she used to describe this process are a testament to the power of visual journaling to solicit the inner truth of one's feelings and the wisdom those feelings reveal. Her statement was so appropriate that Susan began using it to explain to new participants that visual journaling would enable them to go deeper than words could take them, and that in doing so their images would give voice to their souls. Thus the title of this chapter: *Going Deeper than Words to Give Voice to Your Soul.*

Journaling with words (verbal journaling) is the most common method people use to record their thoughts and experiences. We have found that most serious journalers go beyond the mere recording of daily events in an attempt to quench a thirst for that often elusive dialogue in the core of their souls. Unfortunately, as many of those

who have attended our workshops readily admit, they rarely succeed in getting to that core part of themselves with words. A woman in one of our more recent workshops told the group that for years she had kept a written journal even though she knew it didn't allow her to get into the real depth of her feelings. "I'm a writer by profession," she said. "Words come so easily to me that when I use them to journal, I am able to fool myself into writing what I want to believe about something that's happening in my life. Once I started doing visual journaling, the self-deception ended." As Linda Hill-Wall said, "Visual journaling speaks a language deeper than words."

WORDS INTERPRET OUR FEELINGS

Words, which are a left-brain function, make it extremely difficult to get into our core feelings, because the left side of the brain is not an experiencer of our feelings, it is an interpreter. To make its interpretations, the left brain uses the parameters of our individual belief systems. Our beliefs, learned in childhood, dictate our standards of right and wrong, good and bad, acceptable and unacceptable. They determine our expectations of ourselves and others. These beliefs become the measure the left brain uses to analyze, evaluate and judge every experience as it translates those experiences and the feelings they evoke into verbal thoughts and memories. These thoughts are the words we hear inside our heads, the words we speak to others, the words we use when we create a verbal journal. They are the words that tell us what we *think* we feel, which is not always the same as what we actually feel.

For example, when we think we feel anger, we may really feel hurt. When we think we feel love, we may really feel dependence. The problem that arises is that we often base our decisions, choices and actions in life on the thoughts we have about our feelings, which, as you can see, may have absolutely no relationship to our real feelings. Is it any wonder that so many of us have all the things we thought we wanted and yet still feel empty inside?

Words separate us from our feelings. They tell us what we *should* do, while the feelings that tell us what we *must* do often go unheard. To go deeper, to get to the core of our feelings, to get to the heart and soul of a matter, we need to use a different language, a language that by its nature and derivation is not analytical or judgmental, a language that reveals our feelings rather than interprets them. That language is the body-mind's inner imagery.

IMAGERY REVEALS OUR FEELINGS

Imagery is a function of the right side of the brain. Every experience we have and the emotions that accompany it are perceived by the body and the right brain as imagistic sensations. Although any of the senses can produce an imagistic impression, visual imagery, which can be anything from a recognizable object to an abstract shape or color, is usually (for sighted people) the strongest of these sensate impressions. That is why when we feel angry, we often say we see red. When we are sad, we may say we feel blue. Or when we near the end of a difficult ordeal, we may say we finally see a light at the end of the tunnel. These are prime examples of the universal imagery we all share and associate with particular feelings or emotions.

Imagery is also very personal. Every emotion we experience is first expressed as a feeling sensation inside the body before the left side of the brain identifies it, interprets it and translates it into words. Every feeling sensation, including those provoked by emotion, has a corresponding image association that is carried through the body via the sympathetic nervous system. Since no two people experience a feeling in exactly the same way, no two people visualize or draw a similar image for the same emotion. For example, one person may visualize rage as an exploding red, orange and yellow ball of fire, while another person pictures a cold, hard ball of steel. While the first person's image reveals rage that is hot, expansive and directed outward, this same person's verbal description might be nothing more than "My rage felt scary and out of control." This statement tells us very little about this

Figure 1-2. **Painting My Way Out of Pain**, *from the journal of Adele Karbowski*

person's inner experience of rage, since words like *scary* and *out of control* can mean different things to different people.

To illustrate the distinction between expressing an emotion in words and expressing it in images, take a look at the next two journal entries

Frank (a pseudonym) did during his first week in one of our workshops.

Figure 1-3 shows the first page of Frank's journal. On this page, he began by doing what is called a *check-in,* in which journalers write down one or two words that identify how they feel at the moment. They then write down a few more words to explain what it is like to experience this feeling. Frank wrote the word *frustration.* He then described his frustration as confusing, irritating and exasperating.

Unfortunately, as in the previous examples, Frank's words shed little light on the nature of his frustration. Since the next step in the visual-journaling process is to identify one's intention in

Figure 1-3. **Frustration (word),** *from the journal of Frank*

Figure 1-4. **Frustration (image),** *another journal drawing by Frank*

body where he felt the physical sensation of frustration. The image he associated with the feeling was a corkscrew being pushed into a cube of ice that was cracking in all directions.

Frank told the group that this image communicated far more than his words about how he felt. We asked him what his image would say to him if it could speak. "It would say to me," he replied without hesitation, "'You get frustrated because you try to make things happen too quickly. You push too hard and everything begins to crack around you. What you need is patience and trust that you can accomplish more

exploring a particular emotion or feeling, Frank wrote that his intention was to know the source of his frustration. The next page of his journal (Figure 1-4) is a drawing of the image that came to him as he became aware of the place in his

through gentle persistence than heavy pressure.'"

Frank was amazed at the insight his imagery conveyed. "It's so simple," he said. "Why didn't I ever see it before?" He had spent most of his life, he told us, watching his efforts fall apart before his eyes, never understanding that he always tried to force things to happen. He did it in his relationships and with job opportunities. "I never understood why people would give me a chance to move ahead in a relationship or with a job promotion only to turn away from me. I always thought it was them," he said. "And now I see that it was really me. How could I learn so much from one little image? I've been in therapy for years trying to figure all this out." Frank discovered, through his first experience with visual journaling, that images do indeed speak louder than words.

Like Frank, when you learn to connect with your image associations for any emotion you experience using the meditative technique of guided visualization, you discover without a doubt what your real feelings are, rather than what your left brain tells you about your feelings. Also like Frank, when you allow your images to speak to you, they not only reveal the source of your feelings, they often show you just what you need to learn.

ONLY YOU KNOW WHAT YOUR IMAGERY MEANS

The imagery an individual draws or paints is so unique that no one can ever really interpret someone else's artwork. Even when two people experience exactly the same emotion, their imagery (and therefore the meaning of their imagery) will always be vastly different. That is why you can't depend on a therapist to tell you what your work represents. You must learn how to do that for yourself. We will guide you through that process in this book, using self-exploration questions that will accompany each journal exercise.

To demonstrate what we mean, take a look at the next examples of imagery drawn by two people to express the emotion of sadness. Both of these women were in the same visual-journaling workshop. When they began talking about their drawings, it was interesting for the rest of the group to see not only how differently each of them experienced sadness, but also how much their drawings revealed about the nature and source of their sadness.

The journal drawing in Figure 1-5 is by Robin Boyd. She told the journaling group that she had been feeling a lot of sadness throughout the previous week, so she decided to explore that emotion in her journal entry one night. This is what she had to share with us about her drawing: "There are times when I feel so sensitive to the world, like when I see a dead animal in the road, and then I start to feel all the pain in the world. I just don't have any defenses to help me through that, and I've been feeling that a lot lately." When Robin allowed herself to tune into the feeling of that sadness inside her body, she became aware of tension in her heart.

Robin then imagined what that feeling would look like if it were expressed as an image. "The image I came up with," she said, "was these black fingers gripping my heart and not letting the tears out, not letting the sadness out. It created a black hole that I couldn't find my way out of. Then I drew this shape that looked like a conduit that was a place where the sadness could escape and be expressed. And I said to myself, 'No, it's not a closed circle—it goes right off the page and enters the world.'" When Robin shared

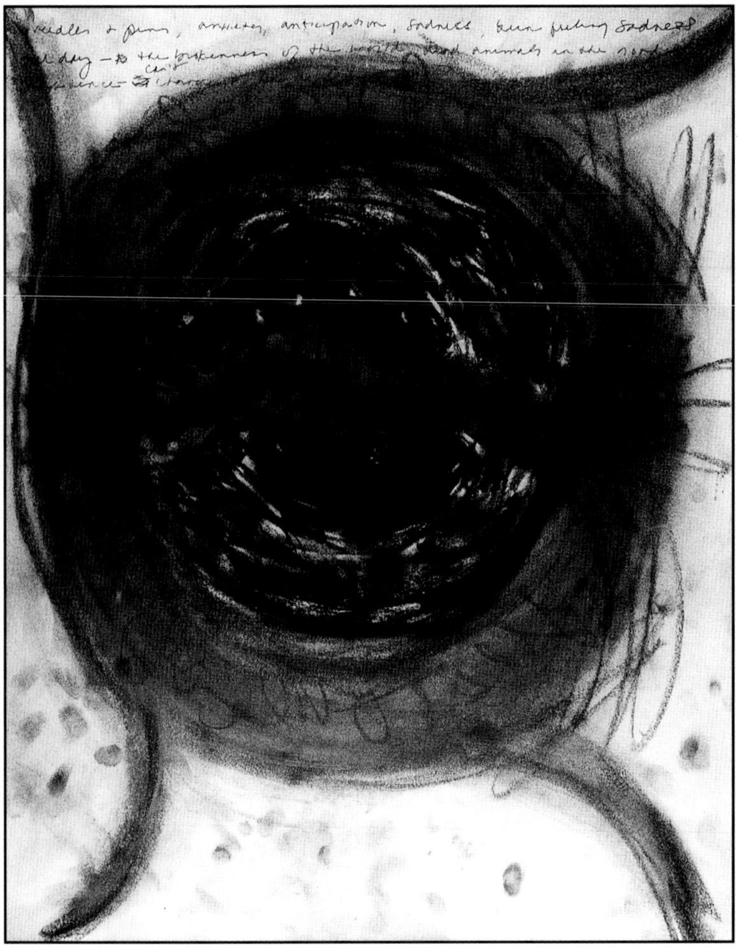

Figure 1-5. **Sadness,** *from the journal of Robin Boyd*

this drawing with the group, we asked her how she felt after completing her journal entry. "Great," she said. "It felt like the sadness really did escape through that conduit. The drawing helped to release the feeling."

Visual journaling is not only a wonderful way to access emotions and feelings words cannot express, it also helps to release those feelings so that you no longer have to carry them around with you.

In the second drawing, Figure 1-6, the other woman, Kyung Kim, began to draw an image of the constant and severe pain she had been suffering for a long time in her neck and shoulder. As she proceeded, she got in touch with a shape that began to form a question mark. When she asked herself what this was about, she told the group that she became aware of a feeling of sadness that she didn't even know was there—deep inside her heart. As she continued to work into the drawing, it evolved into a heart-shaped form. Beneath the drawing, she wrote, "Physical pain: when will it end? Will it ever end? Can I experience anything else deeply with this going on? Can I lose myself in anything else?" When we asked her to talk about what her drawing was trying to tell her, she said, "The sadness and this image are about being unable to participate fully in the world, to be present to my experiences because of this pain. As I drew this image, the first color was red, but then, just below that surface layer of pain, I came to a very blue place near my heart. My sense was that this was a field of mystery, like a question mark. Then I drew an overlay of diamonds."

OUR FEELINGS COMMUNICATE WHAT WE NEED

As we learn to interpret our imagistic language, we also begin to understand what our feelings mean. Feelings communicate needs. They are warning signals when something is amiss within the body, mind or spirit. They let us know when our thoughts and actions are not in harmony. A state of inner harmony keeps us physically healthy, emotionally stable and spiritually attuned to our soul's highest intention. Knowing the full meaning of our feelings can keep us moving on the path our soul was meant to travel. That is the function of the soul's voice: to keep us informed through our feelings and emotions, to impart wisdom that will help us fulfill our divine destiny.

In Robin's drawing, she not only got in touch with the source of her sadness, but also with what she needed to do about it. For her, finding a way to release her feelings of helplessness allowed her to experience a sense of relief, even though she could not change the pain that existed in the world. Although Kyung did not find a way to relieve her pain through her drawing, she did get in touch with an emotion that her pain had created. Becoming aware that her pain was causing a deep, hidden sadness gave Kyung some insight into another part of herself. As she continued working with her journal drawings during the weeks to come, she was able to go deeper into her feeling of sadness, and she eventually connected with what she felt was the emotional source of her physical pain.

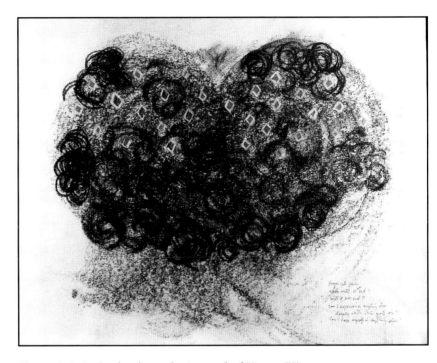

Figure 1-6. **Sadness,** *from the journal of Kyung Kim*

One point that is important to understand when you begin to express an emotion through your journal drawings is that you don't always have to resolve the issue that creates it. Often just the act of getting in touch with how something really feels inside your body—rather than how you *think* it feels—and expressing it, is enough to offer a sense of relief. It is also tremendously freeing to express an emotion without having to deal with the critical judgment of the left brain. The right brain simply accepts our experiences and the emotions accompanying them as valid and necessary.

The right brain, research has proven, is incapable of judgment. It merely records our

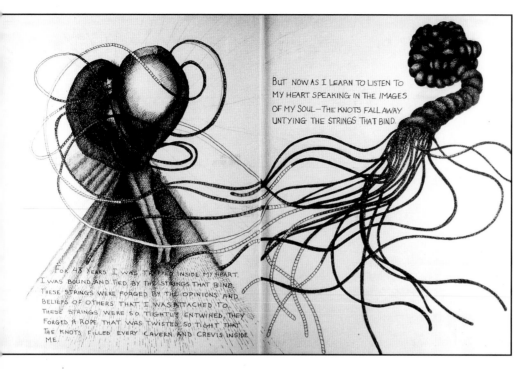

But now as I learn to listen to
my heart speaking in the images
of my soul—the knots fall away
untying the strings that bind.

For 43 years I was trapped inside my heart.
I was bound and tied by the strings that bind.
These strings were forged by the opinions and
beliefs of others that I was attached to.
These strings were so tightly entwined, they
forged a rope that was twisted so tight that
the knots filled every cavern and crevis inside
me.

Figure 1-7. **Trapped inside My Heart,** *from the journal of Barbara Ganim*

reactions as imagistic impressions and perceives them in terms of comfort or discomfort, rather than evaluating them as right or wrong, good or bad. For instance, if we experience something frightening, our imagistic impression of that experience will cause a feeling of discomfort, triggering the body-mind to move away. Meanwhile the left brain may reinterpret that fright as challenging, exciting or daring, and urge us to move toward it. This can put us in harm's way.

Take, for example, a group of teenage boys who think it would be cool and exciting to climb a water tower and walk along the narrow rim. Although each one of them may have a strong right-brain impression signaling them to refuse, their left brain may succumb to their learned belief that it is unmanly to show fear. Thus it is easy to see how following the left brain's judgmental and

sometimes foolish guidance can lead us in a direction that may be contrary to our highest good.

A question so often asked when we use left-brain logic to search for reasons to explain our circumstances, good or bad, is: "Why did this happen to me?" Is it the luck of the draw, a roll of the dice? Or perhaps what Einstein said is true: "God does not play dice with the universe." When we learn how to see beyond what our words tell us and tap into our inner imagery— the language of our feelings and the voice of the soul—we will view ourselves, our world and our experiences in a new way that sees hope instead of desperation, acceptance instead of anger, and possibilities instead of limitations. Our soul wisdom never asks, "Why did this happen *to* me?" It only asks, "Why did this happen *for* me?"

Visual journaling, done on a daily basis, will answer that question as it reveals the life lessons behind all that we do, all that we experience and all that we feel. Visual journaling is the first step in the journey back to feeling without guilt, without shame and without judgment. It is the first step back to rediscovering the wisdom our feelings can provide—the divine wisdom of the soul.

CHAPTER TWO

Taking the First Step

My pictures are my diaries.

—Edvard Munch

Journaling with visualized imagery is a personal journey—one that is filled with adventure, joy and laughter as you rediscover your true nature. We call it *rediscovering your true nature* because what you uncover about yourself, your nature, your desires and dreams, will seem strangely familiar, as if it were something you have always known but simply forgot. In fact, you have always known everything there is to know about yourself and your life's purpose—at a soul level.

The soul's knowledge, we believe, is an eternal guidance system designed to lead us through life and beyond, lighting the way and pointing us in the right direction. Like any guidance system, it sends messages that warn us when danger is imminent or an opportunity is on the horizon. But if the channel through which the messages are sent is blocked, the messages go unheard. That's how it is for most of us. Our soul messages are sent but not received because we often ignore the soul's channel of communication —our feelings and emotions. The journey you are about to embark upon through visual journaling will help you to reestablish that blocked connection.

THE INFLUENCE OF CARL JUNG

Visual journaling has its roots in the early work of Carl Jung, who practiced creating images in his journal every day. He would begin by making small circular drawings in his notebook, which to him seemed to correspond to how he was feeling at that moment. Jung believed these images rose spontaneously out of his instinctual inner world as sacred symbols to lead him to the voice of his higher self.

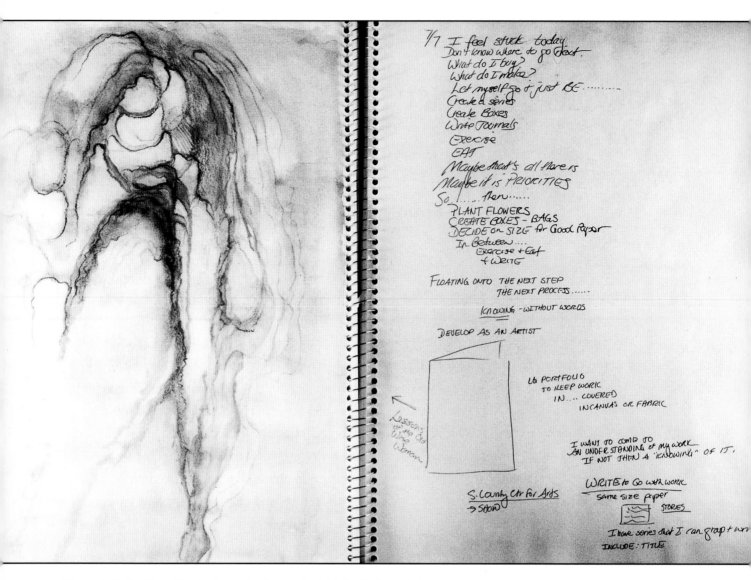

Figure 2-1. **Feeling Stuck**, *from the journal of Adele Karbowski*

PREPARING FOR THE JOURNEY

Before any journey can begin, there are certain preparations that must be made. This chapter will help you prepare for what we hope will become a lifelong pursuit of your inner world. These preparations start with a list of the materials you will need. This is followed by some ideas that will help you set up a work space. Then we take you through the four basic steps of visual journaling that you will use throughout the six-week program outlined in the remainder of the book. These steps are quite simple, and once understood, they will become an instinctual part of your journaling process.

Materials

There are some things you will need to purchase if you don't already have them at hand. Buying art materials is one of our favorite parts in preparing for this journey. Going into an art supply store is exciting and somewhat addictive. If this is a new experience for you, beware: there are more varieties of papers, pencils, pens, brushes, chalks, crayons, pastels and paints than can ever be imagined. So be careful not to get too distracted or excited, otherwise you may be tempted to buy out the entire store. To help you through the temptation, we have simplified the shopping list so that there are only a few things you will need in the beginning. We also suggest some optional materials that can be purchased later when you are ready to experiment with other media.

- An 11" x 14" (or larger) artist's unlined journal or hard-bound pad of drawing paper, or a spiral sketch book (any reasonably good-quality drawing paper in a booklike format will do)
- A box of multicolored pastel chalks (the more colors, the better)
- A box of crayons (the larger, the better)
- An assortment of colored markers with a variety of tip sizes
- A roll of paper towels

This next list includes additional materials that can add variety to your visual-journaling experience:

- A box of watercolors and watercolor brushes of varying sizes
- A box of 12 or 24 colored pencils
- White or clear glue
- Several bottles of glitter in a variety of colors
- Masking tape
- Scissors
- Tempera or acrylic paints in a variety of colors
- A variety of brushes

Setting Up Your Journaling Space

Ideally, your journaling space should be a place that allows you to be undisturbed during the time you set aside for this work. Constant interruptions can prevent you from achieving the focus and concentration that are essential to the visual-journaling process. In addition, the location you select needs to be a place where you can feel safe, protected, nurtured and at peace. Ideally, your work space should be away from the hustle and bustle of family or housemates. It should also offer privacy and some degree of seclusion. An important consideration is being able to leave your journal and art materials out where they will be undisturbed and ready for your next session. Your journaling space does not have to be an area used exclusively for this work, but it does help if everything you need is available when you are ready to begin. Your journaling space can be as simple as a corner of your bedroom or a shady spot under a tree in your yard; it can be an extra room that you set up as a journaling studio. Where you do your work is not as important as the feeling it imparts.

When you have decided on a space, you may want to place some personal objects in it. For example, are there things you have saved or collected over the years that have some special meaning to you, or that are somehow relevant to the exploration of your inner self? Such keepsakes could be anything from old furniture to childhood toys or family mementos. Are there are photographs of certain people in your life who have been important to you? Perhaps it would be comforting or inspirational to include them.

One of our workshop participants spent an entire week redoing a spare room in her house to use as her studio. "Instead of working in my journal this week," she told the group apologetically, "I worked on my journaling space. It seemed really important to have a place where I could close the door and be left alone. The best part about setting up this room," she added, "was that I found an old drawing desk that had once belonged to my aunt, who was an artist. I brought it up and refinished it. Having this desk to work on makes me feel like my aunt is still with me, and that I am keeping her artistic spirit alive."

Have fun as you set up your journaling space, but be aware that you are setting a stage. Walking onto that stage will transform you into another state of being, just as an actor is transformed when the curtain goes up. So make sure that when you choose your space and the things you put in it you create an environment that fosters introspection and self-discovery.

Everyone sets his or her stage differently. One of our journalers likes to have a special music tape playing that is meant to transport the listener out of ordinary space and time. Another person always brings a vase of fresh flowers to her space, while still another folds handmade paper into cups to hold the paint or sand she uses in her work. Take time to think about what is important to you and what would help you to become more deeply immersed in your own inner world. Fill your space with things that envelop your senses, for it is through the senses that your emotions flow, and it is through your emotions that the soul speaks.

One student converted a large walk-in closet into her journaling space. Another student reclaimed a corner of her attic. She was drawn to this space because it had a large window through which she could watch the evening sky. When she first happened upon this corner of the attic, it was filled with cobwebs and boxes of dishes and silverware encircling a dusty, threadbare overstuffed chair piled high with old blankets and quilts. She swept out the cobwebs and donated the blankets to a nearby animal shelter. She used one of the quilts to cover the chair and another to cover the floor beneath it. She salvaged an old bedside table from another place in the attic and

Figure 2-2. An illustration by Barbara Ganim

draped it with a crocheted tablecloth her mother had made. She used it for an arrangement of candles, incense and crystals. She then bought her son a new CD player and used his old portable tape player to record guided visualizations and mood music. This space became a very soothing environment. Most important, she didn't have to disturb anyone in the family to create it.

Even though it can be extremely gratifying to have a special place to do your journaling work, it is not absolutely essential. One of our workshop participants has a sales job that requires a good bit of traveling, so she bought herself a 5″ x 7″ journal book that she keeps in her purse. She says it's great, because she can work on her journal drawings whenever she has a little extra time—whether waiting in her car or in a hotel room.

THE FOUR BASIC STEPS IN VISUAL JOURNALING: DOING A PRACTICE JOURNAL ENTRY

If you have gathered the basic materials and set up your work space, then you are ready to begin the preliminary exercises that will introduce you to the four basic steps in the visual-journaling process. These steps are extremely important, and as much as you may want to jump into the next chapter and begin your visual-journaling work—please resist the urge! You will use these four basic steps each time you work in your journal. They are fairly simple in concept, yet essential in practice. So we suggest you read through each step carefully and then do the accompanying exercises as a practice journal entry, since the first week of the six-week

program begins with the next chapter. If you have never worked with drawing materials before, you may want to keep it simple by starting with pastel chalks.

STEP ONE

Setting a Clear Intention

Before each visual-journaling session, it is important to set an intention that describes what you want from the experience. An intention designates a purpose, reason or goal for what you plan to do. When your mind sets a focused intention, it sends your body a message that there is a clear objective behind the actions you are about to undertake. Your body in turn responds to that message. Setting an intention also combats the interference or resistance that often appears when we challenge ourselves to go beyond our conscious thoughts and judgments.

An important part of setting an intention before you begin is to develop awareness of not only what you want, but what you don't want. For example, if your intention is to express your true inner feelings about an unpleasant experience that occurred that day, then you are clearly conveying a message to your body, mind and spirit that you *don't* want your left brain's judgmental interpretation of that event.

Formulating the words to reflect your intention and writing them down on your journal page before you begin drawing sets up a structure for each journaling session. It also allows you to bypass your left brain's judgments and to clear the neural pathways in your body-mind. This is a necessary step to access the feelings and emotions you wish to express.

Setting an intention can take many forms. As you become more involved in the visual-journaling process, you most likely will develop your own method. It can be as simple as closing your eyes and reviewing the events of the day (if you journal in the evening). If you journal in the morning, you may want to reflect on how you feel at that moment or on feelings that are still with you from the previous day. As you focus on some emotion or event, your intention may then become a verbal statement that you write down on the top of the journal page. That statement might go something like "My intention is to discover the inner source of my feelings about my argument with my boss." Or "I wish to understand why seeing my mother makes me anxious."

Where you write your intention in your journaling book is up to you. Some people prefer to write it on the page preceding the one on which they draw. Others write it on the back of their drawing page. We suggest, however, that you write your intention somewhere near your drawing so that you will know what your drawing was about, should you go back and look at it in the future.

Intentions can also be set through ceremony and ritual. Part of Susan's preparation in setting an intention includes lighting a candle and taking a series of deep breaths. She then writes down her intention, which is always the same: to connect with that sacred part of herself from which she receives soul wisdom. She then affirms, out loud, a desire to be guided by what she refers to as "the

Spirit that moves through all things." If you want to use such an affirmation but the word *Spirit* doesn't suit you, you can substitute *God*, *the Source*, *Buddha*, *the Great Goddess*, or other words that are more closely attuned to your own beliefs. When you use this type of spiritual affirmation, you reinforce the idea that all creation is really a cocreation, a union between yourself and a higher power.

So if you are ready, close your eyes, take a deep, calming breath and ask yourself what your

---

EXAMPLES OF INTENTIONS

These are some examples of intentions that our visual journalers have used for their own drawings:

- I intend to connect with the feeling of tension in my stomach.
- I intend to be open to whatever images want to move through me.
- My intention is to understand the sudden mood swing I am experiencing.
- My intention is to know the truth in my heart.
- I intend to draw the joy and peace I have been feeling lately.
- I feel timid as I start this process; I intend to find out what the source of that timidity is and draw it.
- My intention is to clarify my feelings about my fiancé.

Figure 2-3. From the journal of a workshop participant

intention should be for this practice journal entry. Now relax and take a little time to allow the answer to come to you. Fear not, it will. Then when you know what your intention is, write it down in your journal.

The journal entry by one of our workshop participants shown in Figure 2-3 is an excellent example of just how simple and straightforward an intention can be. This participant's intention, as written on the top of her journal page, says, "I want to know how I'm feeling today." In group, she said that her mind told her that she was feeling agitated, but she didn't know what that

really meant. She couldn't get in touch with the feeling sensation of that agitation. Her intention was to access the imagistic impression her body and right brain were experiencing around this agitated feeling.

STEP TWO

Quieting the Mind through Body-Centered Awareness

If you have completed the first step, you are ready to move on to the second. To get in touch with the feelings and emotions through which your soul voice flows, you must disconnect from your thoughts. This is called *quieting the mind.* Most of us experience our thoughts as a kind of mind chatter that blocks our ability to feel what is happening inside the body. Only by connecting with your body can you access your emotions and the images associated with them, because every emotion is expressed as a physical sensation, and every physical sensation has a corresponding image association. Thus, to access your inner language, you must quiet the source of your verbal language. This can be easily accomplished through what we call *body-centered awareness.*

Body-centered awareness is a technique that allows you to shift attention away from your mind and into a particular part of your body through breathing and simple guided visualization. This exercise facilitates what we all do naturally when we stub a toe or feel an itch, and our attention is instantly drawn to a precise spot on the body.

Take a few minutes to read through the directions that follow, and then try it for yourself. You may even want to read the directions into a tape recorder and play them back to take yourself through each step.

Exercise in Body-Centered Awareness

- Sit in a comfortable position and close your eyes. Take three long, slow, deep breaths and exhale, concentrating your attention on the rise and fall of your chest. Feel the air move in and out of your lungs. Now take three more breaths and imagine yourself breathing in light and breathing out a color—any color at all. Then take three more breaths, and again breathe in light and breathe out color with each breath. Feel your body begin to relax with each exhalation. Continue breathing in light and exhaling color until it feels completely natural and comfortable.

- Now breathe normally, and as you do, allow your awareness to move away from your breathing. Let it drift toward any place in your body that draws your attention. It could be a place where you feel tension or discomfort, or one that feels particularly relaxed and comfortable. If you find that you are not drawn anywhere in particular, just allow your awareness to move into your heart center or any other place in your body where you would like to be more present.

- As your awareness enters that space, focus on that part of your body. What does it feel like to be there? Can you imagine what this part of your body looks like on the inside?

Quieting the mind through body-centered awareness brings you to the state of being where you can begin to see with your inner eye. Step Three will take you further into the experience. Through guided visualization you will begin to access your inner language of imagery.

STEP THREE

Seeing with Your Inner Eye through Guided Visualization

We all have the ability to see with our inner eye. We visualize images when we daydream and when we dream at night. We also visualize images every time we think a thought or feel a feeling. For most of us, these inner images go unnoticed. Our early conditioning teaches us to bypass our imagistic sensations and rely on left-brain, verbal interpretations of our feelings. But occasionally these imagistic messages break through our automatic screening process in the form of an intuitive hunch. Think back to the last time you had an internal signal that told you something was about to happen. Was it a flash of an image or a kind of picture impression in your mind's eye? That's an inner message coming through.

In Step Three, you imagine what the feeling sensation you were focusing on in the previous exercise (quieting the mind) would look like if it were an image. That image might be recognizable, such as a mountain, a face or a rocking chair. Or it could be totally abstract, like a squiggly line or a circle with slashes of color spilling out of it. It doesn't matter what it is or how it looks or if anyone else knows what you are trying to draw. As long as you know what your image represents, then that is all you need.

Exercise in Guided Visualization

- Close your eyes once again, take several deep breaths and focus your attention on your body by feeling the rise and fall of your

HOW PEOPLE VISUALIZE IMAGERY

The students in our workshops often express a concern or even a fear that they won't be able to see anything when they close their eyes. That thought may also be running through your mind right about now. So we'll tell you what we tell them. Don't worry! People experience their inner imagery in different ways. Some don't actually see images, shapes or colors; instead they merely sense them. For others, a certain shape or color may flash through their awareness, not as an actual picture but more like a thought impression or idea.

To get an idea of how you experience your own inner imagery, try this little experiment:

- With a piece of drawing paper in front of you (preferably a piece of scrap paper) and some chalks, crayons or colored markers at hand, close your eyes and imagine a sailboat.
- Now open your eyes and draw the sailboat.

To discover how visualization works for you, ask yourself the following questions:

1. Did the sailboat present itself to your inner eye as a kind of flash image or picture?
2. Did you only sense what it looked like?
3. Did you just begin to draw, having no idea what it would look like until you finished the drawing?

These examples are the three most common ways in which people experience guided visualization. Whichever example was closest to your own way of imagining or seeing the sailboat doesn't matter. The end result will always be the same—you will still be tapping into your right brain, whether you see the image, sense it or just allow yourself to spontaneously draw it.

You might experiment with all of these methods to see how each one feels to you. The most important part of working with inner imagery is to learn to trust your own way of accessing it. If you close your eyes and nothing happens, don't get frustrated and give up. Just start making marks on the paper. Eventually an image will appear. The more you work with visualization, the stronger your connection to your inner imagery will become.

chest. Once you feel connected to your body, allow your awareness to go back into that body part where your attention was drawn in the previous exercise. Focus on the physical sensation in that part of your body.

- Imagine what this sensation might look like if it were an image. If an image doesn't come to you, either as a vision or an idea, then just imagine what colors and shapes or forms would best express it.

STEP FOUR

Drawing Your Inner Images

This final step will show you how to express your body-mind's inner imagery as a drawing. It combines Step Two and Step Three.

- With your journal in front of you, open to the page on which you wrote your intention. Close your eyes again and imagine the image you visualized in Step Three, or the colors and shapes that would best express the feeling sensation you are experiencing in your body. Now open your eyes and draw the image or shapes and colors.

You have just completed your first visual-journaling drawing. How easy was that? Now place your journal on the floor or prop it up on a table or chair, and move back a bit so that you can look at your drawing from a distance. Then sit down and take a good, long look at it. Does it surprise you? How did you come to this visualization? Did you see it as an image with your inner eye? Did you just sense what it looked like? Or

BEWARE OF JUDGING YOUR VISUALIZATIONS AND YOUR DRAWINGS

Be careful not to judge what you see or sense as you visualize and draw, because that will shift you back into the left side of your brain. If you sense that judgment is beginning to take over during a visualization, tell yourself to cancel the intruding thought. Then refocus on your breathing and shift your awareness back to the place in your body where you were previously focusing. Continue with your visualization. If judgment starts to interfere while you are drawing, close your eyes again, get back in touch with your body and your visualization; then open your eyes and continue to draw.

If you still sense yourself being critical or questioning the meaning of your colors or images, draw with your nondominant hand. That will make it impossible for you to be concerned about what your drawing looks like, which in itself will shift you back into the nonjudgmental right side of your brain.

did you simply begin to draw what you knew it would look like? If you read the sidebar, you will know that these are the three main ways in which people visualize inner images. There is no right way to do it. Whatever works for you is right.

Some of you may have concerns about maintaining consistency in your journaling practice, or perhaps you have doubts or fears about your ability to connect with your inner images or draw them. In either case, we recommend that you trust the process and stay with it. After your first and second attempts, we're confident that visual journaling will become an exciting part of your day—a time you look forward to and treasure. The time you dedicate to making meaningful strokes on paper with pastels or moving paint around the surface of your journal page will become irresistible as you connect to the source of life itself—your soul.

This completes your visual-journaling preparations. You are now ready to move on to the next chapter and begin the journey into your inner world.

CHAPTER THREE

Visual Journaling as an Everyday Practice

Traditional methods of prayer and meditation have been elusive for me in the past. . . . For me, painting is my meditation. It is my gift from Spirit, a tool to help me as I journey down all the roadways in this life . . . toward the joyful discovery of who I really am.

—**Jeanne Prom**

INTRODUCTION TO THE SIX-WEEK PROGRAM

Research has shown that prayer, meditation and creating art all have the same effect on the physical body: they alter the brain waves by inducing an alpha state of deep relaxation. Visual journaling, done on a regular basis, will not only serve as a means of self-expression and exploration, it will also help you maintain a feeling of tranquillity, even in the midst of an emotionally charged event in your life.

(Figure 3-1). **Fear of Trust,** *from the journal of Sabra*

To help you develop a daily practice so that you can maximize the benefits of this life-altering process, we have organized the chapters of this book, beginning with this one, into a six-week program. Each chapter presents a specific weekly focus that enables you to move into deeper levels of personal exploration, while at the same time helping you develop your ability to express and understand your imagery.

This approach does not mean that at the end of six weeks you will have learned all you need to know about yourself and be finished with the visual-journaling process. As with any form of journaling, visual journaling is a lifelong endeavor that keeps you connected to your inner self and your soul's voice. Our intention in presenting this six-week program is to offer you a model you can

Figure 3-2. **Hiding the Face of My True Self,** *from the journal of Birgitta Grimm*

"This journal drawing said it all for me—I hide the face of my true self far away where no one can find it. I keep it safe from the storm of criticism that often surrounds me."

adapt into your own daily routine. As you find the most conducive time and place to integrate visual journaling into your day, you will also develop a consistent schedule that suits your personal needs.

When we first began our visual-journaling

workshops, we recommended that our participants set aside anywhere from ten minutes to no more than an hour a day, every day, to work in their journals. Rather quickly, though, we discovered that few people could manage this. Now we suggest that people begin the six-week program by making a commitment to do their visual journaling at least three days a week. What we have found over the years is that three times a week seems to be the average most people settle into after they make the grand attempt to do it daily. It is far better to set a more moderate goal that is easier to achieve than to set a goal that proves too difficult to maintain over the long run. Some people get so frustrated when they fail to live up to their initial expectations that they give up trying to keep a journal at all. Journaling is a way to help you alleviate the stress from your life, not add to it.

WEEK ONE

Accessing and Expressing Your Emotions

For the first week, your focus will be simply to learn how to access and express, through your inner language of imagery, what you feel emotionally each time you sit down to do a journal entry. This beginning exercise is called a *check-in*. Throughout the entire six weeks, we encourage you to do a check-in at least once a week, regardless of the focus you are working on during that week. For those of you who continue to do visual journaling beyond the six-week program—and we hope that is every single one of you—the check-in will become the mainstay of your journaling practice. It enables you to ascertain not only what you feel at any given moment, it can also help you zero in on any life circumstance or issue and discern what emotions they generate.

Check-ins are an excellent way of staying in touch on a regular basis with how you feel. Most people get so busy with work and family obligations that they lose touch with their emotions. We must never forget that emotions surface as warning signals when our lives, thoughts or actions are out of balance and in need of our attention. Contrary to what some people would like to believe, ignoring them doesn't make them go away. They fester and eventually erupt into an even more unmanageable form, such as depression or physical illness. Unresolved emotions will demand our attention in one way or another, and in the end, they always win. Acknowledging our painful, stress-producing, uncomfortable feelings as they occur keeps us physically healthy and mentally tranquil.

(Figure 3-3). A check-in drawing: **Boxed in . . . Trapped,** *from the journal of Sabra*

TIPS TO HELP YOU MAINTAIN A REGULAR AND CONSISTENT VISUAL-JOURNALING PRACTICE

Nearly everyone who begins visual journaling asks these two questions:

1. How can I find the time in an already busy schedule to do my journaling work?
2. How can I stick to my schedule?

The answers came from our longtime journalers. Most of them, through trial and error, finally found a method that worked for them. Here are some of the tips they passed along to us that enabled them to develop a consistent visual-journaling practice that for many of them has lasted years.

- Think about your daily schedule over a typical week, then select a time of day in which you can arrange to be alone for one hour. That may mean talking with the members of your household to get their cooperation and their promise to not disturb you.
- The journalers who are best able to maintain a consistent schedule are those who pick a time when other household members are in bed.
- Think of your journaling time as if you were signing up to take a course outside your home. If this were the case, what would you need to do so that you could attend regularly? Hire a baby-sitter? If so, then find someone to baby-sit for the hour you intend to do your journaling work. Would you need to leave work early several days a week? Can that be arranged? If not, can you find a private space to work during your lunch hour?
- Always schedule an entire hour even though you may not always need it. At least you will have it scheduled.
- Things you may need to do to ensure that you will not be disturbed:
  —Unplug the telephone.
  —Put a DO NOT DISTURB sign on the door.
  —Pick a time of day that is usually less distracting and demanding, such as just before bedtime or early morning before everyone else gets up.
  —Set a clear intention in the form of an affirmation or prayer that reinforces your desire to not be interrupted.
- Don't even attempt to work when your mind is preoccupied with other things.
- If it seems that there are always other things you must do, then you need to decide how important visual journaling is to your emotional and physical health and harmony.

If you decide that it is as important as any of the other things that keep competing for your time and attention, then set up a priority list. Schedule each activity on your calendar and vow to adhere to your schedule.

- From the start, arrange a schedule that is reasonable and easily doable.

- Consistency will help you maintain your journaling schedule. If possible, plan to do your journaling at the same time and the same day each week.

- If while you are journaling something pops into your head that you forgot to do or need to do, write it down and give yourself permission to put it aside until you have finished your work. If it is absolutely crucial to attend to it at that exact time, then do so without guilt, and promise yourself that you will complete your next session without interruption.

- Stick to your schedule as much as possible, but don't condemn yourself when the unforeseeable comes up. The most important thing is to get back on schedule as soon as you can, or reassess your schedule if this one doesn't work.

- Take your work seriously, understanding that it can and will change your life.

- Organizing a visual-journaling support group can help you stay with it. The last chapter of this book will tell you how to get one started.

- Guard your visual-journaling time as much as you would your time with a special friend or loved one. In this case, *you* are the loved one you are making time for.

- Maintaining a consistent schedule sets up a rhythm that, once in action, helps you stay with it.

- Learn to recognize your own subconscious resistance. If you have trouble staying with your schedule, if you keep thinking other things are more important, like cleaning the house, grocery shopping, walking the dog, or weeding the garden, then your subconscious mind may be resisting your best efforts to befriend it. If this happens, confront your resistance—do a journal drawing that expresses what that resistance feels like. Or ask your inner self for a symbol that represents what you need to overcome the resistance.

The check-in, like all the other exercises in this book, is based on the four steps of visual journaling that you were introduced to in the previous chapter. However, as you will discover, the exercises in this book are not all identical. Each exercise is specifically designed to help you explore various aspects of your emotional nature. This chapter contains three different kinds of check-in exercises to get you started with what we hope will become a lifelong practice of visual journaling.

The first check-in is quite similar to the guided visualization in Chapter Two. This will be followed, as will every journal exercise, by a set of self-exploration questions to help you understand what your journal drawings mean. Next will be two more check-in exercises that incorporate movement and sound into the basic four-step process. We developed these two exercises especially for those of you who may have difficulty getting into your body and connecting with your feelings through breathing and visualization alone. They are alternative methods that can be used with any of the exercises in this book. Even if you know right now that using movement and sound does not appeal to you, we suggest that you give these two exercises a try before deciding which format works best. You might just be surprised. All three exercises take you through your first week,

Figure 3-4. A check-in drawing: **Calm,** *from the journal of a workshop participant*

assuming that you journal three times during the week. If you find yourself doing more than three journal entries, you can repeat any one of the exercises.

The Body Never Lies

In these check-in exercises, if you know what you are feeling before you begin, you may want to write it down as part of your intention. For example, you might say, "My intention is to explore my feelings of anger." But if you are clueless about your emotions, don't worry—your body will tell you when you tune in to its signals. As you do this exercise, whatever part of your body attracts your attention is expressing an emotional feeling. The body never lies. It knows, before our conscious minds know, that an emotion is being experienced.

Every emotion begins as a feeling sensation before the left brain or our verbal thoughts tell us what we are feeling. So if your attention is attracted to your solar plexus—that place just beneath the breastbone—and the feeling sensation is uncomfortable and the muscles feel tense or tight, then you are holding an emotion in that part of your body. It could be anything from anger to fear to apprehension or guilt. As you visualize what that tightness would look like as an image and then draw it in your journal, you will begin to get a sense of what that emotion is. But you probably won't know what it's about until you finish answering the self-exploration questions.

As you become more adept at communicating with yourself, the entire process—locating sensation in the body, getting an inner image of it and identifying the underlying emotion—will move much more quickly.

Don't Neglect the Check-In—Even If You Feel Great

Many of our journalers ask us if they should still do a check-in when they feel great. Our answer is always a resounding YES! It is just as important to acknowledge and express yourself when you feel terrific as it is to express your troublesome emotions. Why? Because when you know what images you associate with joy, happiness and contentment, you can use them during times of sadness or depression to help coax your body out of it. (See Figure 3-4.)

Remember, the body-mind responds to an image of an idea before it responds to words that describe that idea. So the next time you feel down, just pull out an old journal drawing of an image that expresses how you would rather feel. Just looking at it may be enough to encourage your body-mind to perk up.

Before You Begin

Pretaping the exercises: You may find it easier to concentrate on the journal exercises if you pretape them, especially in the beginning as you get accustomed to this process. It is much easier to disconnect from your thoughts and focus on your feelings when you don't have to read through an exercise at the same time you are trying to do it. However, if you don't pretape the exercises, then we suggest that you read through each set of directions first, so that you know generally what you need to do. Then silently guide yourself through each step.

Using music: Playing soft background music as you tape an exercise or while you guide yourself through the directions can help you achieve a deeper state of relaxation. Leaving the music on while you draw will help you maintain your focus. It is important, however, to select music that does not have lyrics. Music with words shifts your consciousness back into left-brain, verbal thoughts. Of course, some people find music of any kind distracting. If you are one of these folks, you may prefer silence or recordings of nature sounds such as the ocean surf, a babbling brook, gently falling rain, or chirping birds. Try a variety of music or sounds until you find what works best.

Laying out your drawing materials: Lay out your drawing materials before you actually begin an exercise, so that you can start work in your journal without disrupting the deep state of relaxation you achieve during the visualization phase.

Drawing media that are best for beginning journalers: When people are just learning how to do visual journaling, we encourage them not to use pencils, fine-point markers or pen and ink. Pastels, crayons and broad-tipped markers help keep the drawings loose and expressive. More raw emotion will come through a drawing that has broad, bold lines, shapes and colors than one that is tightly rendered and highly detailed. So in the beginning, especially if you are not familiar with these drawing media, try all three and see which one works best for you. As you begin to get a better feel for the visual-journaling process, you can experiment with other materials, such as water colors, acrylic paints, collage and even mixed media. In the previous chapter (p. 19) we listed all the different types of art media that our journalers like to use, and how these different media lend themselves to various kinds of emotional expression.

Where to write your intention: We recommend that you write your intention on one page and do your drawings on the opposite page.

When you look back at your drawings days, weeks or even months later, it's much easier to remember what they were about if your intention and the images are next to each other. Writing your intention and making your drawings on adjoining pages rather than on the same page gives you extra space to write down your responses to the self-exploration questions that follow each exercise. Again, when you refer to your journals at a later date, it is helpful to have everything together.

Dating your journal entries: It is also wise to date each journal entry so that you know what was happening during that particular period in your life.

EXERCISE #1

The Check-In

Unlike some of the journaling exercises in this book, which may take an hour or more depending on what you put into your drawing, a check-in doesn't have to take long. Once you see how much a few meaningful strokes with your pastels, crayons or markers can tell you about what you are feeling, you will begin to realize that a quick drawing can be just as substantial as a fully developed, detailed drawing.

Some of our journalers tell us that even though they do an hour or so of visual journaling at least once a week so that they can do a more involved drawing or painting, they like to take five or ten minutes every night before they go to bed for a quick journal check-in. It helps them see how they are feeling, especially if they have had a difficult or stressful experience during the day.

They also say they feel better and sleep better because they have been able to express and let go of what they have been carrying around the entire day.

When you are ready to begin your first check-in, open your journal to the next two side-by-side blank pages and follow these directions:

- On one of the pages, write down your intention, which should in some way reflect your desire to discover what you feel emotionally at this moment.
- Next, close your eyes and take several deep breaths, focusing your attention on your body. Feel the rise and fall of your chest as you breathe in and out. Continue doing this until you feel connected to your body.
- Allow your conscious awareness to be drawn toward whatever part of your body attracts your attention. It may be a place that feels discomfort or pain, or a place that feels warm and inviting.
- When your awareness becomes present in this part of your body, concentrate on the physical sensation you feel there.
- Now imagine what this physical sensation would look like if it were an image. What colors, shapes or forms would best express it? If you are quiet and patient, a picture, shape or form of some kind will present itself, either as a visualized image within your mind's eye, or you may just sense the idea of an image.
- When you know how you want to express what this feeling looks like, open your eyes and draw your image on the opposite page of your journal.

- If you did not see or imagine anything during this visualization, then just open your eyes and select a color that best represents what you feel. Allow your hand to move in any way that seems to express what this feeling might look like. As you begin to put marks on your journal page, follow your instincts. They will guide you to add more colors and shapes, and before you know it, an image will appear.

Self-Exploration Questions

Following each check-in drawing, put your journal drawing on the floor or prop it up on a table and study it for a while. Then read through the self-exploration questions that follow. These questions are designed to help you see what your images and colors might mean. As you read through each question, allow yourself to respond intuitively—that is, trust the first response that comes to you. Don't think about it. Don't mull it over. Just answer each question honestly and spontaneously. No one will ever have to see your answers, so let the truth fly. We want to remind you of what we said earlier: only you can know what your drawings mean. You are the only authority when it comes to interpreting your imagery. So trust yourself to know the answers to these questions. Write them on the same page where you wrote your intention.

1. As you look at your check-in drawing, how does it make you feel?
2. What does this drawing tell you about how you feel emotionally? For example, if the colors are dark and cold, could you be

feeling alone and isolated or shut down emotionally? If the image you drew is frightening, is there something you are afraid of? If your drawing is playful and bright, is it telling you that you are happy and full of fun?

3. How do the colors make you feel?

4. Is there anything in your drawing that disturbs you? If so, what? Write a few sentences in your journal about how or why this part disturbs you.

5. What do you like best about your drawing?

Write a few sentences about how this part makes you feel.

6. What have you learned from this drawing about what you feel?

7. Are these emotions related to a particular current issue or concern? If so, what is it?

8. Does knowing what you feel about this issue or concern help you deal with it? If so, how?

Figure 3-5 demonstrates how one of our workshop participants used the left side of her journal to write down her intention for her check-in drawing, and the right side to draw the image

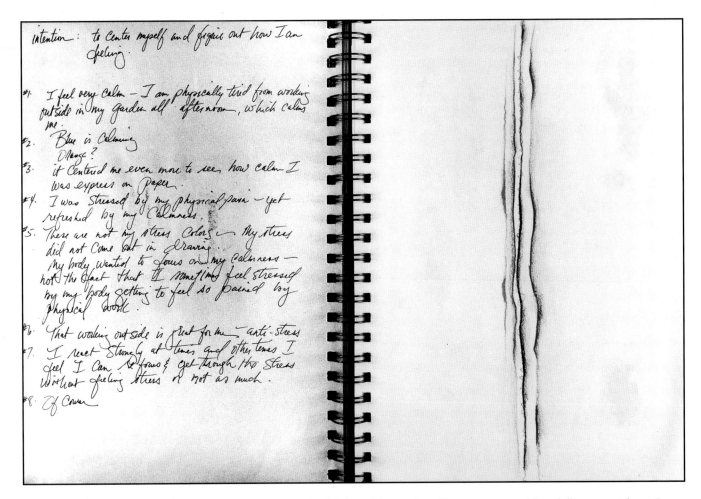

*Figure 3-5. A check-in drawing, from the journal of Sabra. "**Intention: To center myself and figure out how I am feeling.**"*

that represented what she was feeling. Then she went back to the left side to write the answers to the self-exploration questions.

If you found yourself having difficulty answering your own self-exploration questions, take a few minutes to read through Sabra's responses. Knowing what other people feel when they look at their journal drawings can give you some new insights into your own images.

USING MOVEMENT AND SOUND TO ACCESS IMAGES

If you found it hard to shift your awareness from your thoughts into your body in the first exercise, try tapping into your other physical senses. One or both of the next two exercises may help you access your emotions and the images you associate with them by using movement or sound to heighten your perception.

EXERCISE #2

Accessing Your Feelings through Movement

In addition to breathing and focusing your awareness on your breath, moving your body is another way to shift your attention away from your thoughts and into your feelings. Movement is a sensual experience, and anything that activates our physical senses will draw our attention away from our thoughts. We cannot think and feel at the same time—we can be present only to one or the other.

When you are ready to try this second exercise, clear a little floor space where you will be doing your drawing. You may want to try playing some slow, sensual music, as it may help to facilitate your body movements. Then follow these directions:

- Stand near the place where you will be working on your journal drawing. Close your eyes and begin to focus on your breathing. As you become present to the movement of air in and out of your lungs, shift your attention to your feet.
- Bend your knees slightly and slowly twist your body at the waist ever so gently from left to right. As you move, allow your hands to slowly float upward into the air following the movement of your upper torso. Then allow your head and shoulders to begin moving in unison as you continue to twist your torso to and fro.
- Slowly increase the speed until your arms and hands float up to a level almost equal to your shoulders. Do this for a few minutes, and then begin to slow down until you have just about come to a complete stop. Now change directions and begin to twist slowly from right to left. Allow your hands to rise with the movement of your torso. Begin twisting your shoulders in unison.
- Slow down again and allow your body to lazily move or sway, twist or bob in any direction or any way that feels comfortable. Let your body take the lead—it will show you what it wants to do. Continuing moving for a few minutes. Keep your movements slow and gentle, allowing your body to feel soft and malleable. These are called soft movements.
- As you move, feel your attachment to the earth—the weight of your body on the

ground beneath your feet. Let your arm and hand movements become slow and exaggerated as they follow the movement pattern of your body. Try to remember the feeling of this movement—imagine in your mind's eye what it looks like.

• Slowly raise your hands into the air, and allow them to move as if tracing an invisible form. Now pick up a pastel, crayon or marker, and while you are still standing, let your hand trace that same movement onto the journal page. Using the line or form your hand drew on the page as an initial mark, respond to that mark by adding additional lines. These lines are an energetic expression of what you feel inside. This is exactly what we do when we doodle. Every doodle is an expression of an inner feeling.

• Now, while standing or sitting, continue to add lines, forms and shapes to your doodle, changing colors if you wish, until you sense an image coming forward. Ask yourself when you look at this doodle, "What does this remind me of?" As you begin to recognize a form of some kind, help it emerge by outlining it or adding some definition to the doodle. If you have no inkling of a recognizable form or shape in your doodle, just keep drawing and adding to it until you sense that it is finished. You will know when it is done—the drawing will tell you.

When your movement drawing is complete, go back to the previous self-exploration questions and explore what this drawing is trying to tell you.

The journal drawing in Figure 3-6 is an example of a doodle drawing done by Carol Issaco. Carol always uses some form of moderate movement to access her doodles. Once she has drawn the general shape of the doodle, she looks at it to identify a recognizable shape or form within. She outlines the recognizable forms and labels them in the margins of her drawing. In this drawing, Carol saw a kite and a flag, which she outlined in black.

She then closes her eyes and, instead of answering the self-exploration questions, she asks her inner voice—which she calls her "Wise Woman"—to speak to her about these doodle forms. She writes any messages that she receives directly onto her drawing. In this example, Carol's Wise Woman told her the kite meant that she was ready to fly, and the flag meant that she should give herself a hug.

In Carol's second doodle drawing (Figure 3-7), you can see the heart that she identified and outlined. In reference to this image, her Wise Woman told her, "Hold onto the vision, hold onto your heart. . . . Accept the energy and the love." She then sensed another inner voice, which she called her "Healing Woman." This voice said, "Each day do one positive thing—send your poem, send your story, write something every day. Breathe, feel, remain open."

We all have an inner voice—the voice of the soul. It speaks in many forms, through our creativity, our movements and our sounds, all of which emanate from our feelings and emotions. Naming these voices can help us identify which part of our soul's voice is speaking. In Carol's case, she connected not only with the part of herself that conveyed wisdom (the Wise Woman),

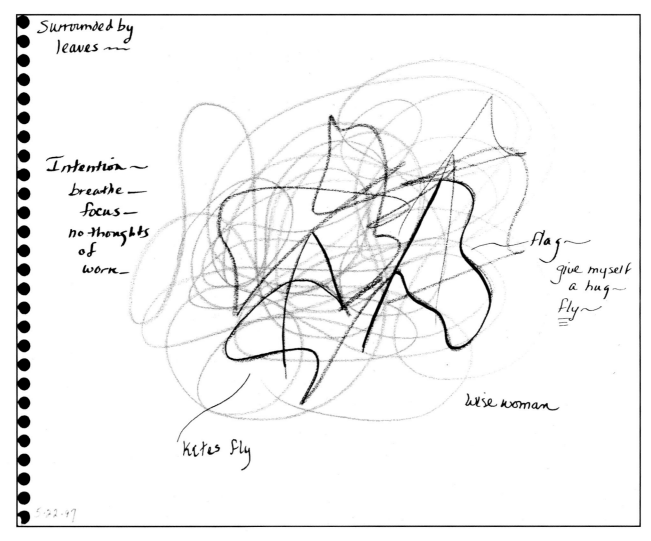

Figure 3-6. Doodle drawing, from the journal of Carol Issaco

but also the part that knows what she needs to heal emotionally (the Healing Woman).

Carol's journal drawings demonstrate how our inner images—whether they are simple doodles or more recognizable forms—are symbolic representations of what we feel emotionally and what those emotions can teach us about ourselves.

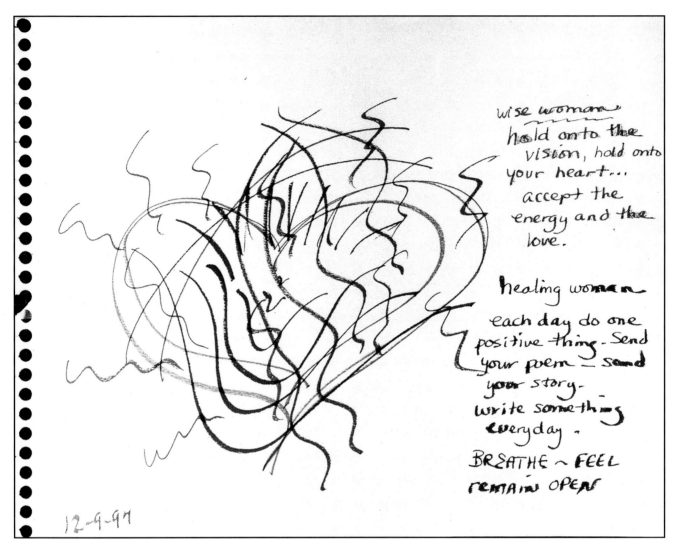

wise woman
hold onto the
vision, hold onto
your heart...
accept the
energy and the
love.

healing woman
each day do one
positive thing. Send
your poem — send
your story.
write something
everyday.
BREATHE ~ FEEL
remain OPEN

12-9-97

Figure 3-7. Another doodle drawing by Carol Issaco

EXERCISE #3

Using Sound to Access Your Emotions

This exercise will help you use sound, in the form of humming, sighing and vocal emoting, to enhance your ability to connect with your body. According to Don Campbell, author of *The Mozart Effect*, sound, music, singing, chanting or vocal emoting are all intuitive expressions of our emotions. Music and sound have a direct effect on both our physical and emotional states by influencing our brain waves, which can activate long-forgotten memories and their associated emotions. In addition, music is a safe way to tap into the many aspects of our unconscious personality and integrate them with the known or conscious personality.

When you are ready to begin this exercise (which you can combine with movement if you choose), follow the directions. It is better with this exercise to forego music, as it may interfere with the sounds your body and voice wish to emote.

- After setting your intention, sit or stand near the place where you will do your journal drawing and close your eyes. Focus your awareness on your breathing, and slowly begin to sigh out each exhalation of your breath. With each exhalation, slowly begin to exaggerate the sound of your sighs. Then let your sighing sound transform into a humming sound. If the hum feels like it wants to take on a particular tune or change tone or pitch, allow it to do so. Continue humming for the next few minutes until you can feel the vibration resonating through your body. If you have difficulty sensing this vibration, place your hand on your throat as you continue to hum. As you feel the vibration resonating into your hand, imagine it moving throughout your entire body.

- As you continue to imagine this vibration, visualize what it would look like if it were a wave moving inside. When you have a sense of what the wave would look like, open your eyes. Select any color pastel, crayon or marker that feels right and draw a line or shape that imitates the wave.

- If the wave form you draw feels like it wants to move vertically or horizontally or in any other direction, allow it to do so. As your hand moves over the page creating lines and shapes, you may notice an image starting to form. If so, continue drawing. Allow the image to develop. If a particular image does not appear, keep drawing your wave form until the drawing feels complete.

When you are satisfied that your sound-wave drawing is finished, go back to the self-exploration questions once again and explore what this drawing is telling you.

DEVELOPING YOUR OWN APPROACH TO THE FOUR-STEP PROCESS

If you have completed the three exercises in this chapter, you probably have a much better sense of how the four-step process works and which method is best suited to you. Once you become comfortable with a particular method, you can then adapt it to all of the other journal exercises. In fact, if you are anything like the other people in our workshops, sooner or later you will begin to develop short-cut versions of the four-step procedure.

Many of our journalers discover after they have been at it for a while that imagining what their feeling sensations look like eventually becomes so natural that they no longer have to go through the body awareness and visualization routines. They just quickly read through an exercise so that they know its focus, and the imagery automatically comes to them. Others say they still do the guided visualization part of an exercise, but no longer write down their intention, because their intention is always the same: to express their soul's imagery or their innermost feelings. So after you have worked with the four-step method for a while, we want you to feel free to alter or shorten it in any way that seems to work for you.

THE PROGRESSIVE DEVELOPMENT OF A JOURNAL DRAWING

These journal drawings, done by two different workshop participants, show the progressive development of an image from start to finish. Each drawing was photographed in four separate stages, from the first marks to the completed journal drawing.

DRAWING #1

Stage One

Jack (not his real name) was the creator of this first set of journal drawings. He began by using the movement exercise to help him connect with what he was feeling emotionally. After several minutes of deep breathing and gentle twisting movement, he started to move his arm back and forth in the air. When he felt ready, he picked up a stick of black chalk. The he lowered his hand to the page and began to draw this initial U-shaped form. When Jack first began to draw, he wasn't completely aware of what he felt emotionally. But within moments of creating the initial shape, he felt his emotions rising to the surface. The U-shape reminded him of a container or bowl that needed some kind of support.

Stage Two

In Stage 2, Jack added a green form beneath the U-shape that made him feel like a hand was gently holding this container.

"That feels better," he said as he was drawing, "more comforting."

Stage Three

After drawing the green supporting shape, Jack became aware that the center of the U-shaped form was attracting his attention. "I sensed that it needed to be filled," he said. So in Stage 3, he drew an egg shape which, as it emerged on the paper, Jack began to fill with color and small circular shapes.

Stage Four

In Stage 4, sensing that his drawing still was not finished, Jack completed the half circle of green, allowing it to enclose the entire egg shape. He then added a light pink around the bottom and sides of the green circle, and gave the curving green line supporting the green circle a more substantial red base.

The drawing now began to feel solid to him, so he felt free to be more playful. "I kind of watched myself in amazement," he said, "as this impishness in me took over, and this snake form

Figure 3-8. Drawing 1, Stage One

Figure 3-9. Drawing 1, Stage Two

Figure 3-10. Drawing 1, Stage Three

Figure 3-11. Drawing 1, Stage Four

emerged from the black surrounding the egg and started to escape. This," he said when the drawing was finally finished, "describes exactly what I have been going through for the last few days, but I didn't know it until now. I haven't been able to acknowledge that I have been feeling empty, scared and definitely in need of support. I have been afraid to ask for help. This drawing tells me that if I do ask, I will get it. And when I feel supported—surrounded by that support—I will feel free to take a chance and break out of my old, going-nowhere-fast circular patterns."

DRAWING #2

Stage One

This second set of drawings was done by another workshop participant who also did not want us to reveal her real name, so we will call her Sarah M.

Sarah began preparation for her journal entry by sitting quietly and focusing on her breath. She then set an intention to connect with an uneasiness she had been feeling for a few days. With her eyes closed, she allowed her awareness to move into her stomach where she felt the physical expression of this uneasiness. As she focused on this feeling in her stomach, she imagined that it looked like an intense black form. She opened her eyes and began to draw that form. While drawing,

Sarah felt the need to push hard to create dark black lines. "The darker the better," she said. She kept the form small so as to not expand the feeling. As she drew, she began to sense that the black form was connected to a feeling of being criticized.

Stage Two

In response, Sarah drew green stick figures of the critical people in her life and then put a barrier of green between herself and them.

Stage Three

When Sarah looked at her image, she felt that it needed something more. Without knowing exactly what that would be, she reached for a piece of brown chalk and found herself drawing a

Figure 3-12. Drawing 2, Stage One

Figure 3-13. Drawing 2, Stage Two

thick circular line around the forms. She noticed then that this brown circle, which was open on two sides, created a sense of safety for her. She also noticed that she had left an opening in the thinner green circle. "This opening feels important," she said, "because it leaves space for me (represented by that black form), to leave."

Stage Four

The more Sarah looked at her drawing, the more she realized that the form looked like a wheel turning. She liked that sense of movement, so in this final stage she drew arrows to exaggerate it. Then she added what she described as dancing stars and little circles. This gave her a wonderful sense of being free from the onslaught of other people's criticism. "That heavy feeling of uneasiness lifted," she said. "As it did, I also felt some pain release itself. To show that release, I drew a black ball floating outside the large circular shape. It joined the dancing stars."

After she answered the self-exploration questions, Sarah realized that her drawing was telling her that although she couldn't stop people from criticizing her, she could choose how to react. "I could continue to feel stuck and bombarded by their criticism," she said, "or I could choose to protect myself by separating and moving away from them. If I moved away and let their opinions go, I would be free—free to dance with the stars."

Figure 3-14. Drawing 2, Stage Three   *Figure 3-15. Drawing 2, Stage Four*

These two sets of journal drawings clearly illustrate how powerful this process is. And as you have discovered for yourself by now, your inner images not only tell you what you are feeling, they also tell you what you need to do about those feelings.

This concludes your first week of visual journaling. We hope you have discovered that creating art, like meditation and prayer, can indeed open doorways to the deepest parts of your psyche, where self-knowledge and self-acceptance cultivate an inner harmony in which body, mind and spirit can thrive.

In the next chapter, you will learn about the importance of recognizing and releasing stress-producing emotions. You will then learn how to transform the image of a stress-producing emotion into a new image that not only helps you feel more positive and peaceful, but also enables you to reverse the harmful effects of stress on your body.

CHAPTER FOUR

Healing Your Stress-Producing Emotions

Visual journaling for me is about taking ownership of my life in a loving way. I've spent much of my life . . . being nice, putting others' needs first, not knowing my needs or listening to that little voice inside me.

—**Kate Siekierski**

Figure 4-1. **Sometimes When I'm Stressed, I Feel Invisible,** *from the journal of Kate Siekierski*

How often have you heard people say, "I have too much stress in my life," as if stress were a weed growing out of control in their gardens? Stress is not a condition that germinates by itself. We create stress when we respond to the pressures, demands and expectations of others in a way that conflicts with our own needs, desires and expectations. In its simplest terms, stress is nothing more than a conflict between what our thoughts tell us we *should* do and what our feelings tell us we *want* to do. The conflict between thoughts and feelings triggers emotional reactions like anger, guilt, fear, frustration, worry and resentment, to name just a few, that activate what is called *the stress response.*

The stress response is a physiological, biochemical reaction that causes the release of hormones that affect the central nervous system. The central nervous system responds by altering our bodily functions to prepare us for the well-known fight-or-flight syndrome. The end result is

tightness in our muscles, shallow breath, sweaty palms and a pounding head. We feel weak, disoriented and shaky all over. Rarely, however, are we able to identify the life event that sparks a stress-producing emotional response. Most people don't even know that they are experiencing a stress-producing emotion until they are called upon to get in touch with it.

The stress response can be activated by two things: a perceived threat to our physical safety or a perceived threat to our beliefs, needs, wants, desires, possessions and well-being. What we call day-to-day stress is usually not provoked by attacking tigers or stampeding elephants, nor is it generated by events such as muggings, car accidents or plane crashes. These dreadful occurrences are usually only once-in-a-lifetime ordeals. The kind of stress most of us face on a recurring basis involves incidents that bring into question our learned patterns of behavior, our beliefs about circumstances that have occurred or our fear that they might occur, or preconditioned thoughts and reactions to the actions and requests of others.

For example, when we are asked to do something that conflicts with our beliefs, like sneaking into a movie, hurting someone intentionally or lying, we begin to feel uncomfortable. This sparks the stress response —we want to fight or take flight. When we are asked to accommodate ourselves to the needs of others and their needs severely contradict our needs, our emotional reactions often go beyond discomfort. We might respond with anger, resentment or even hatred. We also experience the stress response when someone cuts us off in traffic or pushes in front of us in a supermarket line, because this challenges our innate need to be seen, acknowledged and recognized by others.

This need to be seen is aptly illustrated by Kate Siekierski in her journal drawing, Figure 4-1, entitled *Sometimes When I'm Stressed I Feel Invisible.* Kate's comment in the opening quote of this chapter states that she has spent a lifetime trying to be nice, putting the needs of others first and not being in touch with her own needs. What

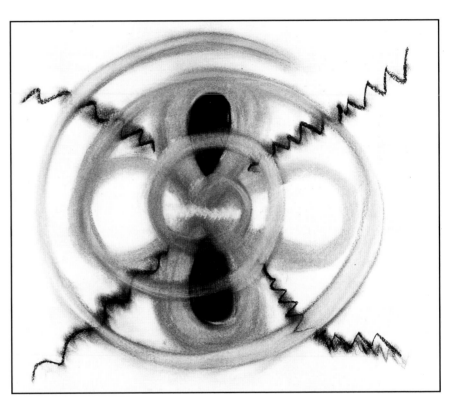

Figure 4-2. **What Stress Looks Like,** *from the journal of Kate Siekierski*

Kate has endured for most her life is exactly what many of us also experience. We keep doing what others want us to because we just don't know what *we* want.

It is only through our feelings and emotions that we can ever know what we need and want.

Our thoughts can't tell us because they have been influenced by learned beliefs that preach doctrines that induce us to bend to the will of the tribe. This sounds noble in theory, but it can be detrimental to our own highest good, and what is detrimental to our highest good is ultimately detrimental to the good of others. Ignoring what we need, what is best for us—not by others' standards and opinions, but by our own—also makes us feel invisible—invisible to ourselves. Thus, being out of touch with our emotions is the primary reason we so often succumb to the will of others, which inevitably causes emotional reactions that generate the stress response. These reactions are *stress-producing emotions.*

While stress-producing emotions can wreak havoc with our lives, the good news is that if we pay attention to them, they can teach us how to connect with the needs and desires we have been ignoring. Then we can make visible those parts of ourselves that have gone unseen, unacknowledged and unheeded. Recognizing the hidden parts of ourselves enables us to become the persons we were born to be. Without our painful experiences and the stress-producing emotions they elicit, we might never discover our strengths and assets—the very qualities we need to accom-

plish what we were brought into this lifetime to fulfill. When we finally understand what our painful experiences and emotions are trying to teach us, the wounds they inflict begin to heal. Only from this new perspective can we see that our worst enemies have been our greatest teachers. With this knowledge comes forgiveness, forgiveness of ourselves for the way we have reacted and forgiveness of those who have hurt us, because without their intercession—painful as it may have been—we would never have discovered who we really are.

How Stress-Producing Emotions Affect Your Physical Health

Research in psychoneuroimmunology, which studies the impact of emotions on the central nervous system and the immune system, has proven that painful emotions that go unresolved and unexpressed for long periods of time have a direct and measurable effect on the immune system and the development of illness and disease. To demonstrate this relationship more clearly and simply, we have developed what we call *the stress equation* to illustrate how unexpressed emotions can produce physio-

---

THE STRESS EQUATION

Unresolved, unexpressed painful emotions = physiological stress =

immune system dysfunction, degeneration of body systems,

and abnormal cell growth + time = illness and disease

logical stress and eventually affect your body.

Of course, it is important to remember that every time you have a stress-producing thought or emotion, you're not going to make yourself ill on the spot, because time is the most important factor in this equation. We all have stress-producing emotions that we may carry with us for days, weeks and even months, but if we have an outlet that allows us to eventually release them, the body can recover. If we do not have an outlet, however, then the continual onslaught of stress eventually creates a weakened physiologi-

cal environment in which disease and illness can more easily develop.

Researchers have also been studying the use of guided visualization, imagery and art as means to reverse the devastating effects of stress on body and mind. The results of these studies show that expressing one's stress-producing emotions through drawing, painting or any form of art can reverse the stress response, which in turn relieves the body of tension, alleviates pain and boosts immune-system functioning substantially.

Through our own work with cancer patients

Figure 4-3. **Blue Armor,** *from the journal of Sabra*

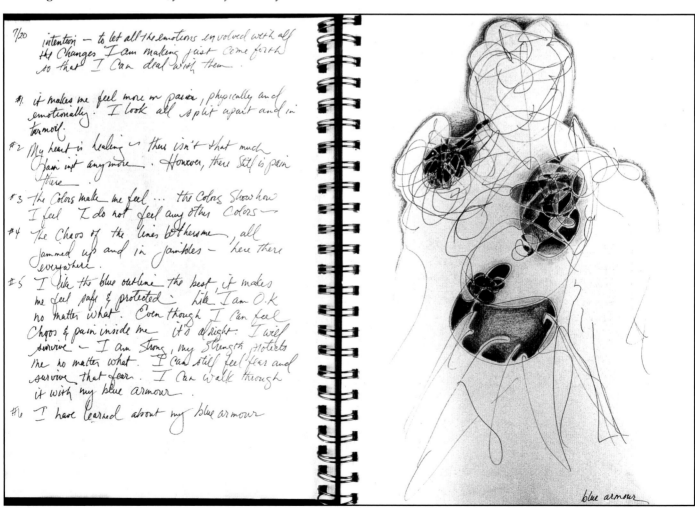

A while back, a woman came to see Barbara because she was feeling stressed out at work. Barbara asked her to begin keeping a visual journal so that she could track and explore her stress as it occurred. Her journal drawings quickly revealed that the stress was prompted by feelings of anger and resentment toward her job as a high school English teacher. She had gone into teaching at her parents' urging when she graduated from college, because they saw it as a steady and reliable source of income. She hated it right from the start, but she stayed with it through the years because she and her husband needed her income to pay bills. It also allowed her, once they had children, to be home after school and during the summer. Now in her fifties, she continued to stay with the job because of her accumulated pension funds.

When she began to look at her stress from a different perspective, she realized that what she really wanted to do was to open a little antique shop. Antiques were her passion. Denying her passion caused her to resent the time she spent at school, to the point where anger and frustration were her constant companions. And the worst part was that until she began expressing those feelings in her journal drawings, she didn't even know the what or why of them. All she knew was that her job was stressful, and she felt she could no longer endure it. After working through the reasons for her stress, she was then able to address her fear of leaving her teaching position.

Her journal work, she believed, helped her do this. "My drawings not only told me what I wanted to do," she said, "they also helped me to trust my own inner messages that somehow knew exactly what was right for me. I finally learned that my pension was not as important as my peace of mind. And the joy and enthusiasm I have had since I left teaching has enabled me to make far more money than that pension could ever give me."

and others suffering from various types of physical illness, we have found that the act of expressing a stress-producing emotion through drawing or painting enables one to energetically move an emotion outside the body where it can no longer activate the internal stress response.

Although most of the people who take our workshops are interested in better understanding themselves and their feelings, there are always a number of participants in each new group who wish to use visual journaling to help them heal life-threatening illnesses or chronic physical conditions. Those who maintain a consistent journaling schedule of at least three times a week over a period of several months tell us that visual journaling enables them to recover more rapidly from their illnesses, and reduces the side effects of medical treatments. Many of them are convinced that visual journaling is responsible for actually reversing the physical manifestations of their condition altogether.

But regardless of what your own reasons may be for doing visual journaling, the most important thing to understand—whether you are struggling with an illness or not—is that everyone experiences stress-producing emotions from time to time. These emotions must be released on a regular basis in order to keep the immune system operating at peak efficiency and to reverse the powerful effects of stress on the body. Visual journaling is without a doubt one of the best ways to release stress-producing emotions, while at the same time enabling you to delve into the innermost depths of your soul.

WEEK TWO

Accessing, Releasing and Transforming Your Stress-Producing Emotions

Your focus for this second week of visual journaling is to concentrate on stress-producing emotions caused by current, ongoing life issues. You will also examine stressful, unreleased emotions from the past that still affect you today. As you focus on these emotions, it is essential that you not just express them, but that you go one more step into the phase called *transformation*.

Transformation is part of what we call *the three stages of healing with art.* These are access, release and transformation, or ART.

The first stage involves accessing emotions through body-centered awareness and guided visualization. The second stage occurs when you release these emotions through an artistic medium, such as drawing, painting, sculpture, writing, dance/movement or sound and music. This kind of artistic expression has come to be known as e*xpressive art* or *healing art*. It is used in hospitals to facilitate physical healing and by psychotherapists to help people heal their emotional wounds.

If you have been doing the exercises thus far in this book, then you have already experienced the first and second stages in this healing process. In your first exercise this week, you will continue to use the first two stages of access and release to work with stress-producing emotions. Then we will give you another exercise to help you transform them through a process we call *re-envisioning*. This involves transforming the earlier image of stress-producing emotions in the first exercise into a new image that expresses the way you would like to feel and react as you deal with your stressful experience.

Transformation does not necessarily help us to solve a stressful issue, but it does enable us to look at it differently. That alone can often help us let go of our old and perhaps unrealistic expectations of how life should be. This in turn can encourage us to embrace a new perspective that helps us to explore the soul lesson behind every painful situation. When we transform a stress-producing emotion into a feeling that encourages us to react in a loving, accepting and positive way, we begin to heal our wounds. Thus, painful emotions lose their power over us, and the negative physiological effects of stress likewise heal.

WHAT TO DO IF YOU ARE NOT EXPERIENCING STRESS RIGHT NOW

If you are not experiencing stress, discomfort or emotional pain in your life right now, just continue doing the basic check-in exercise as in the previous chapter until a stressful situation appears. But remember, just because you are not aware of feelings of stress does not mean that you are stress free. Many people become so accustomed to feeling apprehensive and anxious that it seems normal to them.

Our suggestion is that you take the time to do this exercise. When you get to the body-centered awareness part of the guided visualization, instead of focusing your attention on a stress-producing emotion, allow your attention to be drawn to any place in your body where you notice tension or tightness. Or you can ask your body to guide you to where you may be holding stress. If you are patient, your body will comply with your request.

EXERCISE #1

Discovering the Source of Your Stress-Producing Emotions

Have you been feeling stressed, tense, frightened, upset, nervous, anxious or frustrated lately? We all go through periods when everything seems overwhelming and we feel emotionally distraught. Sometimes we can't even identify a specific emotion—we just feel stressed. This exercise will help you get in touch with your own feelings so that you can pinpoint the exact emotions that are being aroused. At the same time, you can discover the source of your stress—which may not be what you think it is.

When you are ready to begin this exercise, which you can combine with movement and/or sound if you choose, follow the directions below.

- Set your intention to reflect what you would you like to know about any stress-producing emotions you presently feel, or any issue that causes you stress. If you are not sure whether you feel stressed right now, ask your body to guide you to any place where you may be holding stress. Then write this intention in your journal.

- Sit in a comfortable position and close your eyes. Take three long, slow, deep breaths, concentrating on the rise and fall of your chest. Feel the air move in and out of your lungs. Next, take three more breaths and imagine yourself breathing in light and breathing out a color—any color at all. Then take three more breaths. Again, inhale light and exhale color. Feel your body relax with each exhalation. Continue breathing in light and exhaling color until it feels completely natural and comfortable.

- Breathe normally. Allow your focus to move away from your breath, and let it drift toward the place or places within your body where there is tension, stress or discomfort.

WHEN WORDS APPEAR WITH YOUR IMAGES

Every time we run one of our visual-journaling workshops, there are always several people who feel as though they are not doing their drawings the right way because words somehow keep emerging from their images. We always reassure them that there is no right or wrong way to do this process; there is only the way that feels right to them.

Figure 4-4. Enough, *from the journal of Bre Churchill*

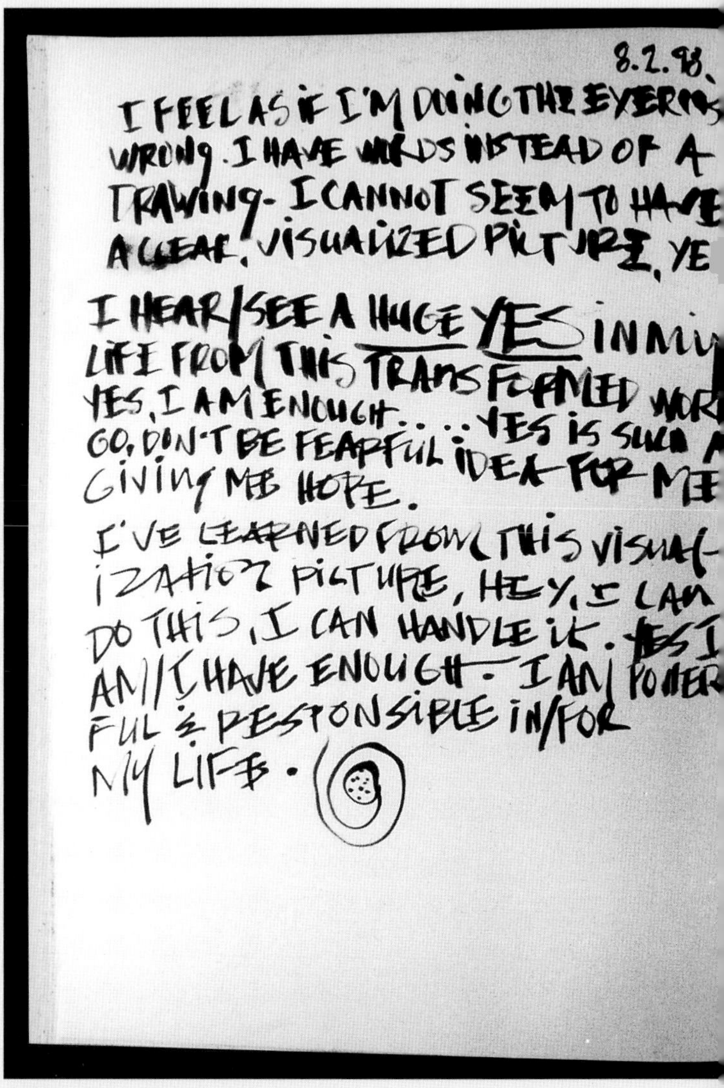

Figure 4-5. Yes, Enough, *from the journal of Bre Churchill*

Bre Churchill's drawings (Figures 4-4 and 4-5) demonstrate her concerns about the words rather than images that keep coming to her during the visualizations. She shared her

apprehensions with the group when she began to talk about these two drawings.

She explained that in her first drawing she was attempting to deal with a recurring stressful

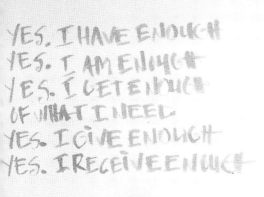

instead—the word *enough*. It was inside a jagged-edged blue form, outlined in red. Then I saw all these other *enough* words surrounding it. This can't be right."

"In the next drawing," she continued, "as I was attempting to transform this stressful image of *enough*, again I pictured a word, only this time it was the word *yes*. That led me to respond to the word *yes* with more words, like 'Yes, I have enough,' and 'Yes, I am enough.' As I wrote the words, I saw a red circle that I think symbolized a feeling of transformation for me. It meant that, yes, there is enough. But then as I answered the self-exploration questions, my fear reappeared. I was convinced that I was doing this exercise wrong."

Bre finally resolved her own misgivings as she answered the self-exploration questions. She went on to write, "I've learned from this visualization picture, hey, I can do this, I can handle it."

Of course, as we pointed out to her in the group, this final statement appears to have a double meaning. It seems to also imply that she can handle thinking of herself as being enough and taking responsibility for her own life. Bre agreed. She said that her fears about both concerns—doing the exercises right and being enough—were finally put to rest with this journal entry.

issue. That issue, she told us, was feeling like she was "never getting enough."

"But when it came to envisioning an image," she said, "I didn't get one. I got a word

Let your awareness be drawn into the physical sensations surrounding them.

- What colors, shapes, forms, or images best express what the physical sensations feel like? When you know, open your eyes and draw your feelings of stress.

After you have completed this drawing, spend several minutes looking at it from a distance as you did with the earlier exercises. When you are ready, answer the self-exploration questions that follow. They will help you to understand the source of your stress and what it may be trying to teach you. You need answer only those questions that apply to you and your situation. If you think of other questions you would like to ask yourself, answer those as well.

Self-Exploration Questions

1. How does this journal drawing make you feel when you look at it?
2. How does the stress-producing emotion you focused on in this drawing feel now?
3. How do the colors you used relate to what you were feeling?

Figure 4-6. **Stress Overwhelming Me**, *from the journal of Sabra*

4. Look at the image you drew. Is there anything about it that bothers you?

5. As you look at your drawing, does it hold any special message or meaning that relates to your feelings of stress? If so, what is it?

6. What have you learned from this drawing about your reactions to stress-producing emotions?

7. How do you feel about the reaction that you expressed in your drawing?

8. Would you like to change the way you react when stress comes into your life? If so, describe how.

If you answered yes to question eight, then follow the steps outlined in the next exercise, "Transformation through Re-Envisioning." It will help you transform the image you drew in the previous exercise into a new, more positive image, one that expresses the way you would rather feel when faced with stressful circumstances.

The journal drawing in Figure 4-6 depicts Sabra's image of stress as a heavy load of boxes crashing down upon her head. It is interesting to see the words she used around her images that further define her stress. They include: "Tears of

Figure 4-7. **Transforming My Stress,** *from the journal of Sabra*

fear," "Pain in Shoulders" and "My heart gets all twisted with fear & feelings of unworthy ness [sic]." The statements she wrote on the opposite page of her journal in response to the self-exploration questions allow us to see how these questions helped her to understand the source of her stress and how she was reacting to it.

Some Journalers Don't Always Use the Self-Exploration Questions

In Figure 4-7, Sabra transformed her feelings of stress by drawing an image of herself releasing the boxes. On the opposite page she wrote a few paragraphs interpreting this new, transformed image. When Sabra brought her drawing into group the next time, she asked us if it was okay that she hadn't used the self-exploration questions. "Sometimes," she said, "I just know what the drawing is about, and I don't really need the questions." Our reply was that the questions are meant to serve only as an aid. Now we want to pass this same message on to you.

The more experience you acquire with your journal drawings and the self-exploration questions, the easier it will be to understand what your imagery means. Eventually, like Sabra, you too will no longer need the questions. However, when you find yourself at that point, we suggest that you still take a few minutes after each drawing to write at least a few sentences about what your imagery means. As you will soon discover, this is an extremely valuable part of the visual-journaling process.

Sabra's transformation drawing is a good example of what can happen when we allow ourselves to re-envision a new, more positive image that expresses the way we would like to respond to our stress-producing emotions. The message Sabra gleaned from her transformed image and then wrote on the opposite page in her journal is an important lesson to us all. Part of that message reads as follows: "I have a choice when it comes to burdens—either carry them and be weighted down or throw them away and transform them into a light part of my life. Balance your life into what you want and need— do not carry unnecessary baggage."

EXERCISE #2

Transformation through Re-Envisioning

Transformation is the process of changing from one state of being into another. When you experience a painful, confusing or anxiety-provoking situation, you may react in a way that is negative, angry, hostile or abusive to yourself or others. These nonproductive reactions generate stress-producing emotions. Most of us simply learn to live with stress-producing emotions, waiting them out, believing they will dissipate with time. The problem is that stress-producing emotions may appear to dissipate over time, but they never go away. They continue to affect us emotionally and physically until we make a conscious effort to acknowledge, release and transform them into a reaction that is more constructive.

For the most part, our emotional reactions, either positive or negative, are learned. When we react in a way that disturbs ourselves and others, we can always choose, like Sabra, to react differently. But consciously and cognitively choosing a better reaction is not enough to sustain change. To make a lasting alteration in our behavior, change must take place on three levels: the conscious, subconscious and cellular. The most effective way to reach all three levels is to use the body-mind's inner language of imagery, which directly activates the sympathetic nervous system—the initiator of the stress response. Since every emotion generates a corresponding inner image, when we alter the image, we alter the response.

This exercise will help you to re-envision— to see differently—your image of your stress-producing emotion as a transformed image that represents a more constructive and positive reaction.

- Set your intention to re-envision a new image that expresses how you would like to feel when you experience the emotional reaction that triggered your internal stress response. Write this intention in your journal book.
- Close your eyes. After a few deep breaths, bring your awareness back to the place in your body where you first experienced the feelings of stress and tension that elicited the previous image.
- Ask your body to present you with a new image that feels less stressful, more positive, constructive and healing. Be patient as you allow this re-envisioned image to come into your awareness. When you have a new image, open your eyes and draw it.
- If you do not actually see or sense a new

image, just open your eyes and draw something that feels soothing and healing.

Your new image represents an emotional transformation, a new way of reacting to a painful or stress-producing experience. It may also convey a message from your soul—a message that can help you understand the lesson behind the stressful situation. That message may be readily apparent. If not, the following self-exploration questions may help you clarify it.

Self-Exploration Questions

1. How do you feel about your new trans-formed image?
2. What message do you sense about what you need to do to deal with stress in a more positive and soothing way?
3. What have you learned about yourself from this second drawing?

During this second week of visual journal-ing, we recommend that you do these first two exercises at least twice to explore—and hopefully heal—any stress-producing emotions you may be presently experiencing.

EXPANDING YOUR JOURNAL WORK BEYOND THE CONFINES OF YOUR JOURNAL PAGES

Some of our journalers say that they simply cannot confine themselves to the journal page. They may start out working in their journals, but then discover an almost uncontrollable urge to work larger. One journaler told us that quite often her emotions feel so powerful and expansive that she needs a much larger working surface. To accommodate some of her oversized images, she tapes several pieces of 18″ x 24″ drawing paper together on the back side, and then flips them over to draw on the untaped side. Other jour-

Figure 4-8. **The Gift,** *from the journal of Sandi Gold*

nalers like to work in three-dimensional media such as clay and wood.

So if you find yourself inspired to convert one of your journal drawings into a large painting or sculpture, if the emotion you are trying to express cannot be adequately portrayed in a journal-size drawing, or if a two-dimensional surface will not do it justice, then let yourself go. By all means, express yourself in any format that feels appropriate. There are no rules when it comes to visual journaling.

The Gift (Figure 4-8) is a wonderful example

of what can be done with a journal drawing when we allow our intuitive instincts to guide us. Sandi Gold started working in her journal one day after her computer crashed in the middle of an important deadline. She felt so much frustration and anger that she needed to find a way to express it.

"I took my markers," she said, "and I just went at it, trying to get out the frustration. I kept going until I felt my anger finally coming out. It was scary for me to let that much anger out, so I knew it was time to transform those feelings. When I asked myself what I needed in order to transform them, something told me that I had to find a box. I didn't know why I needed this box, but I found one anyway, wrapped this drawing around it and taped it. I realized that it looked like a present. I studied this package, and I could still see all the energy in the drawing. That's when I understood that I am this very passionate person and that passion is my gift."

The energy, anger and frustration that Sandi put into her drawing, she told us, was exactly what she had been feeling her entire life because she was so different from her family. She felt at times as if she were an embarrassment to them. As a result, she too became embarrassed by her passion. Expressing the anger allowed her to release this embarrassment and transform it into a gift that she could treasure. This was an important message for Sandi and a real turning point in her life as a professional artist.

If Sandi had squelched the urge to convert her drawing into a box covering, she might never have experienced this transformation.

DISCOVERING YOUR UNHEALED EMOTIONAL WOUNDS

Something else happened when Sandi created *The Gift*. In addition to getting in touch with the source of her anger and frustration, she also got in touch with an old, unhealed emotional wound that still exerted a powerful influence on her day-to-day emotions and reactions.

Most of us are not even aware that the stress-producing emotions we experience are often set off by unhealed emotions from the past that still, as they say, "trip our triggers" and "push our buttons." In such instances, the current stressor unconsciously reminds us of an old feeling we have never resolved. Our reaction to this present-moment event then combines with the aggravation and hostility of long ago, which has now resurfaced. The end result is that both emotional reactions—the one from the past and the current one—have joined forces to deliver a two-fisted punch.

We all have emotional wounds that were never addressed at the time they were first inflicted. Sometimes the pain was so great that we repressed them, reinterpreted them or ignored them altogether. But that did not make them go away. Emotional wounds continue to fester if they are unexpressed and unreleased. So the work you must do now, in addition to expressing your current stress-producing emotions, is to go back and uncover those old, long-buried emotions. The next two journal exercises in this chapter will help you connect with and extract any unhealed emotional wounds that still plague your life today.

EXERCISE #3

Accessing, Releasing and Transforming Unhealed Emotions from the Past

- Set your intention to focus on an unhealed emotional wound from the past that is ready to be accessed and released. Write your intention in your journal book.

- Sit in a comfortable position and close your eyes. Take three long, slow, deep breaths and exhale, concentrating your attention on the rise and fall of your chest. Feel the air move in and out of your lungs. Now take three more breaths and imagine yourself breathing in light and breathing out color—any color at all. Take three more breaths, and again inhale light and exhale color with each breath. Feel your body relax with each exhalation. Continue breathing in light and exhaling color until it feels completely natural and comfortable.

- Return to normal breathing. Allow your attention to move away from your breathing and let it drift toward the place or places in your body where you sense you may be holding an unhealed emotional wound. Your body and subconscious mind will guide you.

- As you are drawn to a particular location, wait patiently and allow yourself to be totally present in this part of your body. Shortly you will notice an emotion welling up inside you. Ask your body to present an image of what this unhealed wound is about.

• When you know what that image is, open your eyes and draw it. If an image does not appear, just open your eyes and ask your drawing hand to guide you as you start putting marks on the paper.

When you have completed this drawing, spend several minutes looking at it. When you are ready, answer the following self-exploration questions. They will help you to understand what this unhealed emotion from the past is all about.

Self-Exploration Questions

1. How does this drawing make you feel when you look at it?
2. Does it call forth any old memories or feelings? If so, what are they?
3. What emotion does your drawing appear to express?
4. What do the colors tell you about the old, unhealed emotion?
5. As you look at your drawing now, does it hold any message about what you were meant to learn from the original experience?
6. Do you sense any similarity between the emotion(s) expressed in this drawing and the present-day stress-producing emotions you drew in Exercise #1?

7. If this drawing could speak, what would it say to you?
8. What have you learned from your drawing about your unhealed emotion?

EXERCISE #4

Releasing and Healing Old Emotional Wounds

Now that you are in touch with this old emotion, would you like to release and heal it? If so, then follow the instructions in this two-part exercise.

Part One

• Set your intention to release this old emotion. Write it down on a new journal page.
• Close your eyes, take several deep breaths, and imagine how it would feel to release this emotion. What image would best express what releasing it once and for all would feel like?
• When you know what it looks like, draw it on the same page on which you wrote your intention.
• When you have completed this drawing, write a few sentences that describe what it feels like to let the emotion go.

Now that you have released it, you can allow the wound to heal. This can be done by re-envisioning a transformational healing symbol to replace the image you drew in Exercise #3. Follow the instructions in Part Two.

Part Two

- Set your intention to transform and heal the old emotional wound. Write it down on another new journal page.
- Close your eyes, take several deep breaths, and allow your awareness to move into your heart center. Ask your heart to present you with a healing symbol that will replace, within your body and mind, your image of the unhealed emotion.
- When you know what your heart's healing symbol is, draw it on the same page on which you wrote your intention.

You may want to remove these last two drawings from your journal and tape them to a wall or leave your journal open in a place where you can look at both drawings every day for at least a week. Repeatedly looking at the image symbolizing your intention to release the emotion and the symbol that represents healing will consciously and subconsciously replace the image of the old emotional wound. These two new images will then activate your sympathetic nervous system to respond with healing endorphins.

Throughout the remainder of this second week of visual journaling, continue using these last two journal exercises to connect with any other unexpressed and unhealed emotions that you may still be harboring. In time, as you begin to rid yourself of these old emotions, you will find that they no longer control your reactions to present-day situations.

As we close this chapter, it seems appropriate to end with a journal drawing, Figure 4-9, *The Letter A* by Birgitta Grimm. This drawing expresses Birgitta's re-envisioned image of her

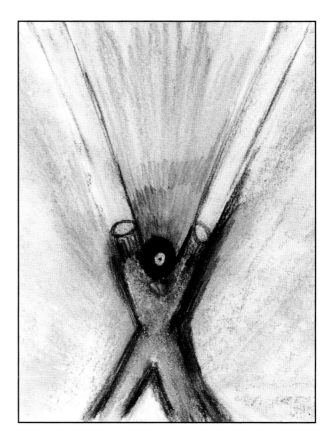

Figure 4-9. **The Letter A***, from the journal of Birgitta Grimm*

stress being released. Upon completing it, Birgitta spent some time dialoguing with her image. She invited us to share with you the message she received. "Let the stress out. There is no need for you to feel this much stress. It can shoot up or down out of the body. There is freedom when your feelings of anger or sadness are fully expressed and released. When this happens, you will be filled with peace and joy once again."

Dialoguing with an image means to ask it to speak to you. The amazing thing is that, when given an opportunity and a voice, your images will speak, just as Birgitta's did. In the next chapter, you too will learn how to dialogue with your own images and, in doing so, give voice to your soul.

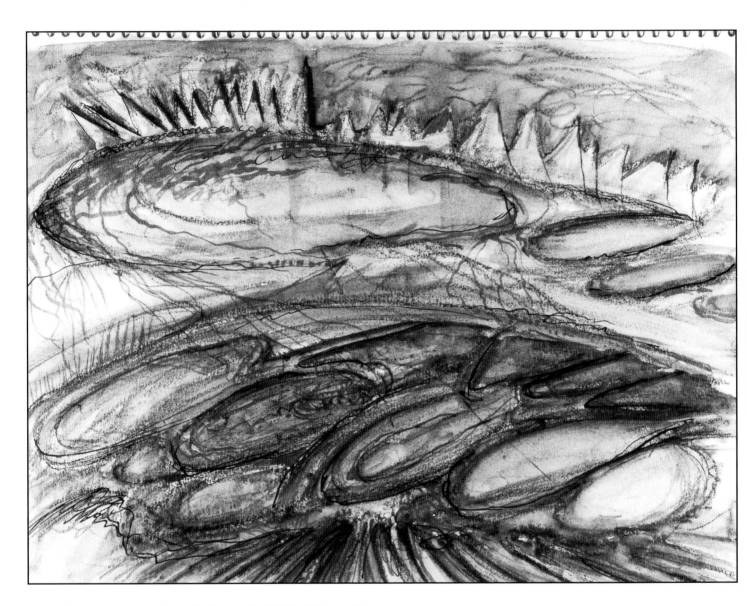

Figure 5-1. **Pods,** *from the journal of Adele Karbowski*

"My painting is full of the same elements I've used before—pods, circles, stringing lines, exploding lines, hills, rocks and shells. But this time I asked my painting where these forms were going, and why? The pods spoke: 'We represent old ways of being, the release of old forms, colors, ideas, and beliefs into unlimited possibilities.'"

CHAPTER FIVE

Conversing with Your Images

I have been doing visual journaling for two years, and I have found that my imagery understands all the emotions in my body. It is my teacher.

—Donna DiGiuseppe

Conversation with an old friend who knows us well can be a cherished experience. We feel an endearing tenderness when a treasured friend speaks to us of times past, lessons learned and memories shared. When we ask this friend for advice, we know it will be gentle and given with our best interests at heart. And so it is when we invite our images to speak with us—to give advice and tell their stories. Like an old friend, our images will converse intimately and with wisdom. And most important, they will connect us to a deep inner voice that can help us rediscover the essence of who we really are.

The voice that comes through our images when we express them in drawing, painting or sculpture is the voice of the soul. To better understand how this voice speaks through our images, think of it this way: Imagery is the language of body, mind and spirit; art is the voice of that language. When we reconnect with that voice, it tells us not only how we feel in response to any life event, but also what we need to do in order to survive and thrive when faced with difficult circumstances or decisions.

WEEK THREE

Letting Your Images Speak

During the first two weeks of this visual-journaling program, while you have been learning how to access, release and transform your inner language of imagery, you have also been learning how to interpret its messages to your body and mind, messages that will help heal the deep inner wounds that have kept them separate for so long. As with any new language, there comes a time when you are able to move beyond interpretation into the realm of inter-personal communication.

You have now arrived at that point; you are ready to begin conversing with your images, to ask questions and receive answers. Sometimes the answers will come in the form of quick, direct responses; at other times they may be entwined in a story, poem, allegory or fable. Therefore, the focus for the third week of visual journaling will be to learn how to converse with your images. To get you started, the exercises for this week are divided into two parts.

In Part One, you learn how to dialogue with any journal drawing using a specific set of questions. From there you are encouraged to develop your own questions. If you have difficulty receiving answers, we introduce several different methods our journalers use that enhance their ability to connect. We also show you how to ask for more insight or further clarification when the message seems ambiguous.

In Part Two, you learn how to let your images reveal their messages. Every image expresses a part of your inner self that has an important story to tell. That story reveals thoughts, memories and desires that may have gone unrecognized and unacknowledged for years. When you learn how to weave a story from your images, you uncover your inner strengths in the form of your story's hero. You expose and learn how to protect your vulnerabilities as you become acquainted with your hero's trials and tribulations. Through the villain, you unveil the dark and hidden parts that must be recognized and brought into the light. These stories from the core of your soul empower you to transform your life into full awareness of who you truly are and the person you were meant to be.

One of our longtime visual journalers, Rob Blais, received some valuable information when he dialogued with images he produced during a check-in session. The painting, *Through the Clearing* (Figure 5-2), shows two houses. "The house in front," Rob told us, "looks strong and secure, but the one in the back doesn't. Because the lines are disconnected, it looks as though it could be crushed easily. So I asked my painting what these two houses meant. This is what it said: 'You have two houses in your life. One house is in order and one is in disarray.' I knew exactly what this meant," Rob said. "It meant that my everyday, material life is together, but my spiritual life is not. The second house represents my spirituality, and it is not cohesive; it needs work. With this answer, some of the questions I had about my life suddenly became crystal clear."

PART ONE

How to Dialogue with Your Images

It is not at all difficult to dialogue with your images. As we said in the beginning of the chapter, it can be just like talking with an old and trusted friend. All you need to do is think of a question you would like to ask either your images or the drawing itself. Write that question in your journal. Then simply close your eyes and allow yourself to remain totally open and receptive as you wait for a response. It will come in the form of an intuitive thought or notion. If you are like most people, you may hear a little voice in your head actually saying the answer. However, we constantly have to encourage our journalers to trust the first response they receive, and to resist the urge to second-guess it. (Experience has taught us that the first response is the voice of the soul; the second is the voice of the head.)

Figure 5-2. **Through the Clearing,** *from the journal of Rob Blais*

ANSWERS TO QUESTIONS ABOUT DIALOGUING WITH IMAGES

As we have said before, many of our first-time journalers begin as skeptics, so we always get our fair share of questions. We share with you now some of those questions and their answers.

Q. What if the voice in my head is just my own voice answering me?

A. The voice you hear *is* your own. It is the voice of your inner self or soul, which is where your images come from. When you ask a question of an image or a drawing, you are not asking a disembodied entity. You are asking yourself—the creator of your images.

Q. What if I find that the responses I receive are critical, judgmental or scolding?

A. The answers you receive from your images are coming from the right side of your brain—the part that thinks imagistically—which is incapable of judgment. That is exactly why the first response is always the right response, because it is coming directly from the right brain. If the answers you receive feel critical, judgmental or scolding, then you have somehow shifted back into the left brain, perhaps by second-guessing your initial response. Remember, the left brain is the seat of critical thinking and judgment.

The solution? Hold your pen in your left hand as you await or write your response. What does that do? It activates a shift from your left brain into your right brain, because your left hand is controlled by the right side of your brain. If you are naturally left-handed, then use your right hand to write the question, then switch back to your left hand to write the answer. That too will activate a brain shift.

Q. What do I do if I get absolutely no response when I ask a question?

A. If you find that your mind is an absolute blank, even when using your left hand to respond, then try writing anything that feels even remotely relevant. If that yields nothing, then try a circular doodle to get yourself started. It has been our experience that words will soon start to flow. You just have to keep your mind very open and receptive. And remember, do not allow yourself to think about an answer. That will shift you back into your left brain.

Q. What if my responses feel contrived?

A. Contrived means artificial, made up. Try this

technique: Ask your question, then close your eyes. Allow your awareness to move into any place in your body to which your attention is drawn. That particular body part is in some way connected with the question you asked. With your focus on that spot, ask *it* for a word or words that relate to the response you are waiting to receive. If words do not come, then ask this part of your body to present an image or a symbol that stands for a word. When you get something, write it down and see if it triggers a sentence.

Q. What if nothing works?

A. If all of these jump-start techniques fail, try different questions. It has been our experience that when we ask our images—which come from within ourselves—a question, we consistently receive an answer, providing that we have asked the right question.

Q. What if the response I get is not at all what I expected?

A. Give up your expectations. Keep in mind that when we ask a question of our imagery, we seldom get what we expect on a conscious level. We do, however, get what we expect unconsciously, because the unconscious is where our responses come from.

Q. What if I still find that the responses I get seem like they have nothing to do with my question?

A. Try asking a few more questions or wait a day or two and then go back to the response. Quite often, after some time has passed, a second reading brings new understanding to a previously confusing response. Finally, if all else fails, take a breather for a few days and then come back to it. You may be trying too hard. Patience, acceptance and trust are the key to communicating with your imagery.

Q. How many questions can I ask my drawing or images?

A. As many as you want.

Q. How do I know which image to start with when I ask my first question?

A. It doesn't matter where you start. Just trust your instincts. We suggest that you start by asking the drawing as a whole what *it* is has to say to you. Then select any image, preferably one that draws your attention or confuses you, and ask that image to explain itself.

EXERCISE #1

Dialoguing with Your Images

We recommend that you begin this week with a check-in drawing to see where you are emotionally. When you complete that drawing, use the questions that follow to help you dialogue with your images.

If you are ready to begin your check-in, open your journal to the next two side-by-side blank pages. Feel free to use movement or sound.

- On either the left- or right-hand journal page, write down your intention, which should in some way reflect your desire to discover what you are feeling emotionally at this moment.
- Next, close your eyes and take several deep breaths, focusing your attention on your physical body by feeling the rise and fall of your chest. Continue doing this until you feel connected to your body.
- Allow your conscious awareness to be drawn toward whatever part of your body attracts your attention. It may be a place that feels discomfort or pain, or one that feels warm and inviting.
- When your awareness becomes present to this part of your body, concentrate on the physical sensation you feel.
- Now imagine what this sensation would look like if it were an image. What colors, shapes or forms would best express it? If you are quiet and patient, an image, shape, form or idea will present itself.

- When you know what this feeling looks like, open your eyes and draw it.
- If you did not see or imagine anything, open your eyes and select a color that best represents what you feel. Allow your hand to move in any way that seems to express what this feeling might look like. As you begin to put marks on your journal page, follow your instincts. They will guide you to add more colors and shapes, and before you know it, an image will appear.

Dialoguing Questions to Elicit Responses from Your Drawings

Your imagery is not only a graphic representation of how your body-mind experiences a feeling, it is also a message from the core of your being telling you what can be learned from these emotions. In order to understand the complex nature of your messages, use the questions that follow to ask for more information from your drawing and its components, such as colors, shapes, forms or textures.

- Write question 1 on the journal page opposite your drawing. Close your eyes and imagine that your drawing is taking on a life of its own. Imagine that each image is coming alive. Now focus on the drawing or the specific part of the drawing to which you posed your question, and imagine what it would say in response.
- Do this with each question. Feel free to improvise, change or add your own questions as you go along.

1. Ask your drawing what it is trying to tell you about yourself or your life through its images, forms and colors.

2. Pick one image—something that attracts your attention either positively or negatively— and ask it what it is doing in your drawing.

3. Select another image, color or form. Ask the same questions as the two above until you have dialogued with every part of your drawing.

4. Look at each answer. If it feels important, you can go deeper by asking for more clarity or insight.

5. If you would like to explore the possibility of a relationship between the messages you received and any other present or past circumstances of your life, then the following questions may help you:

   • At what other time in your life have you had a feeling or emotion that was similar to the one you expressed in this drawing?

   • What life trends or personal behaviors do you sense may be related to the message you received?

   • Is there a particular response to any of the questions you have already asked that might apply to a current situation?

   • Is there a particular response that might apply to a past situation? If so, how?

   • What have you learned from this drawing that may relate to who you are or who you are meant to be?

As you attempt to go beyond the surface meaning of your drawing's responses into a potentially deeper one, try to see the images as a guiding force, a pilot light that warms your heart

and accesses the energy of life itself. When these messages from your soul feel like an earth-shattering truth or an eye-opening "Ah-ha!", you will know that you have completely understood their fullest meaning.

DIALOGUING WITH THE DRAWINGS OF THE PREVIOUS TWO WEEKS

Once you get the idea of how to dialogue with your images, go back and use the dialoguing questions with the journal drawings you did during the previous two weeks, especially the ones involving your stress-producing emotions. These may be particularly interesting and informative—their messages could have a direct connection to the feelings and emotions you express this week.

SEEING YOUR IMAGES AND THEIR RESPONSES AS SYMBOLIC MESSAGES

You may not always understand the responses you get. Interpreting a particular response may require looking at it symbolically; that is, instead of taking the response literally, imagine what the message might symbolize. Rob Blais certainly did that with his painting (Figure 5-2) when he recognized that the houses symbolized aspects of both his material and spiritual lives.

Another one of our journalers, Cherie, could easily understand the symbolic meaning behind her journal drawing, *Mountains* (Figure 5-3), but what she really wanted to know was what advice the drawing could give her. Before she did any dialoguing, Cherie jotted down what she thought the images symbolized in reference to her emotions when decisions were taken out of her hands or life felt out of control. "At times like this, it feels as though there are tall mountain peaks I must climb. Some are dark and shadowy,

Figure 5-3. **Mountains,** *from the journal of Cherie*

"This is how I feel when decisions are taken out of my hands or life feels out of control."

but the middle one is lighter, less threatening. The sky is ambiguous—it looks like it could turn into a raging storm or lighten up into a beautiful sunset. The valleys are green and lush with lots of light."

From a symbolic perspective, it was quite clear to Cherie that her imagery symbolized the

uncertainty she felt when faced with circumstances that could yield unknown outcomes. The mountains and the sky symbolized the difficult climb she anticipated as she navigated through a storm that might or might not come. The valley symbolized respite, a place of comfort that existed below the ominous surface of her mounting fears. But this was not enough. Cherie really wanted to know what her imagery said about the way she handled uncertainty. In an attempt to gain more insight, she did another drawing (Figure 5-4), which she called *Roller-Coaster*.

In *Roller-Coaster* Cherie's intention was to figure out how to deal with her feelings. When she finished studying her drawing, she wrote the following impressions in her journal, once again looking at her images as symbolic messages: "My feelings look like a roller-coaster. There are ups and downs in browns, blues and dark oranges. I seem to be using a lot of dark colors to express unfathomable emotions. The red circles—are they confusion? The misunderstanding of emotions? Out of the center is this bright light that overcomes all the ups and downs and circles. The circles even start to transform into light." Still, there were no definitive answers, so this time Cherie decided to dialogue with her drawing. She asked questions and recorded them in her journal—and her drawing responded.

Question: What is the message of the roller-coaster?

Answer: Why do you get on it when you don't even like roller-coasters?

Question: How do I *not* get on?

Answer: Stay in the center with the sun.

Question: How?

Answer: Just do it.

Question: I'm afraid I won't be living unless I'm on the roller-coaster.

Answer: You're happier and lighter when you are not on the roller-coaster.

When Cherie first reread the responses, she did not understand what they meant. Then she looked at them as symbolic messages. That is when it all began to make sense to her. She told us, "I know that the roller-coaster symbolizes my emotional ups and downs. So I think my response, when I said, 'I'm afraid I won't be living unless I'm on the roller-coaster,' means that I am so used to living with emotional upheaval that when I do allow myself to be in a place of peacefulness and acceptance—symbolized by the light—it's so unfamiliar that it feels frightening." As soon as she said this, Cherie not only knew that her interpretation was correct, she also knew what her drawing's message implied when it advised her to stay in the light. The light symbolized trust. When life seemed out of control, if she allowed herself to trust that things would work out in a way that

was best for everyone, the emotional upheaval would end.

After dialoguing with her roller-coaster drawing, Cherie went back and dialogued with the mountains in her first drawing. She asked the mountains what they wanted to tell her about

Figure 5-4. **Roller-Coaster,** *from the journal of Cherie*

how to get through her fearful times. The mountains replied, "The choice is yours! You can choose to see us as ominous, a dark presence. Or you can choose to see us as a presence that is not dark. Everything around us has possibilities—not just dead ends. The skyline is a choice as well—it could represent dark storm clouds or the possibility of an absolutely gorgeous sunset. The valley always exists as your safety net—it is the part of you that is the core, the essence, the part that belongs to God. It is the spiritual side of you that will flourish no matter what is happening in the material world. It is your haven. The choice is yours! How do you want to perceive the mountains and the stormy skies? Remember, the valley is always there. It has always existed, exists now, and always will, forever."

Cherie said that the message from her images gave her strength, reminding her of her connection to God and to her own inner resources, which included her ability to make different choices. Choice is a powerful gift that we often forget to use. When we journal with images and then allow them to speak, they will always remind us of our gifts, our hopes and our dreams.

PART TWO

Letting Your Drawings Tell Their Story

Every journal drawing has a story to tell. Each image represents a character, and each character represents a different part of yourself that yearns to be seen and acknowledged. Recognizing these previously hidden or unnoticed parts enables you to integrate their desirable qualities into your personality and to learn from their fears and insecurities. Both positive and negative attributes contribute to your becoming your complete self, fulfilling your soul's intention in this lifetime.

Allowing your artwork to tell its story is different from dialoguing with your images. Your imagistic dialogues are intimate conversations, but your stories are tales that may be filled with drama, conflict, and moral dilemmas woven together from the symbols and images you express in a journal drawing. They reflect your soul's knowledge of the inner struggles you will face throughout your life as you attempt to unlock the mysteries of your vast potential. As author Natalie Goldberg often says when she lectures to groups on writing their stories, "Our bodies are garbage heaps. We collect experiences and from the decomposition of the thrown-out eggshells, spinach leaves, coffee grinds and old steak bones of our minds come nitrogen, heat and very fertile soil. Out of this soil blooms our poems and stories."

So get ready; you are about to empty out your own personal garbage heap as you create a journal drawing with an important story to tell.

EXERCISE #2

Drawing with a Story to Tell

Your body will guide you to a story that wants to be told. Where there is physical tension or discomfort, you will discover a message or lesson waiting to be expressed in the form of a fable, allegory, myth or poem. To access this story, you must first become present to the part of your body where this idea or notion literally aches to get your attention. Once you recognize this place, you can invite it to share its images. Use the story-prompter questions that follow this exercise to help you envision the story.

Open your journal to the next two side-by-side blank pages. Again, feel free to use movement or sound with this visualization.

- On either one of the two journal pages, write down your intention, which should reflect your desire to receive images that will tell a story your body longs to express. If you wish to work on a specific issue or emotion, ask to be guided to the place in your body that holds the true story of this issue or emotion.
- Close your eyes and take several deep breaths, focusing your attention on your body. Keep your intention in mind. Feel the rise and fall of your chest as you breathe in and out in long, slow breaths. Continue breathing deeply until you feel totally connected to your body.
- With your intention foremost in your mind, allow your awareness to be drawn toward any part of your body where you sense a feeling of discomfort, tension or pain.
- When your awareness has become present to this place, concentrate on the physical sensation and invite it to share the images that will tell its story.
- As these images emerge, open your eyes and draw them in your journal.

STORY-PROMPTER QUESTIONS

These story-prompter questions will help you give voice to each image in your drawing. As their voices emerge, they will suggest a story. The questions can be used in one of two ways: You can actually record the answers in your journal and then write the story they have prompted, or you can simply read through the questions and write a story from the impressions, thoughts and ideas that arise.

If you have trouble getting your story started, try one of these old-fashioned opening phrases: *Once upon a time*, or *Long ago and far away*, or *One day there was . . .*

1. Write down whatever you know about the images in your drawing or just think about them. What do they mean to you? What are they saying? What do they want you to know about them?
2. Imagine a voice coming from each image. What does the voice say? Write it down or just try to remember it.
3. As you look at your drawing, which image is your main character—the one telling the story?
4. What is this character's name?
5. What do you know about it? Use your intuition to guide you. Is it male, female or without gender? Is it an animal, vegetable or mineral? Is it human or nonhuman?
6. What characters do the other images represent? Is there a hero? A victim? A villain?
7. Do you sense that these characters have names? If so, what are they?
8. What do you know intuitively about these other characters?
9. Look at your drawing once again. Are they in a specific type of environment? For example, is it day or night? Indoors or out? In this world or another world? What season does it seem to be? Is the environment cold and hostile or warm and welcoming?

Based on what you thought about or wrote down as you read through the questions, write a story about these characters. Remember, there is

SUGGESTIONS ON HOW TO INTERPRET YOUR STORY

*E*very story has a message. Your story is no exception. But the message may not be readily apparent. Like the dialogue responses you received when you asked questions of your drawing and its images, the message of your story should be viewed as symbolic of something you need to know about yourself, your life or the way you respond to events or circumstances.

The following questions may help you see the symbolism in your story. You can write the answers in your journal or read the questions to yourself and see what insights they offer.

1. Does this story feel like it is related to a particular part of your life or an issue with which you have been struggling? If so, what is it?

2. What was the main character's challenge or concern? Does it have anything to do with your life? If so, in what way?

3. If there were other characters in the story, did they represent hidden, unknown or unrecognized parts of yourself? If so, what parts?

4. Was there an outcome to the story?

5. Was there a message for you in this outcome?

6. What is the symbolic message of the story?

7. Does this message have any personal meaning? If so, what is it?

8. What have you learned from this story about yourself, your life or your way of handling things?

---

an absence of planning in the creative process. Allow the story to emerge without censoring yourself or planning the outcome. Just let it flow and see what happens. Learn to embrace the unknown. It is the void where creation begins.

Once your story is complete, resist the urge to edit, judge or rewrite it. You may obscure the true meaning behind it. Each story symbolizes, just as your dialogue did in the first exercise, something important that you need to know.

This exercise is a form of indirect communication with the different parts of yourself; each

character is another aspect of you. The story itself puts your beliefs and life events into the larger context of your life journey. It presents a more complete picture than the myopic view we all tend to have when we perceive events from the inside as a participant. When you dialogue with your images, you are part of the experience represented by the images. As the writer of the story, you step outside your images and observe the dialogue and emotions behind the action. Your unconscious mind opens to reveal a sacred vision that reflects your life from the soul's perspective.

PUTTING IT ALL TOGETHER: DIFFERENT WAYS TO APPROACH WRITING A STORY

There are always different ways to approach writing a story from a journal drawing. Although most of our journalers begin by using the story-prompter questions, many eventually develop their own shortcut methods. We have included three examples to demonstrate the various ways our journalers have allowed their stories to evolve.

Some stories emerge as soon as the drawing is finished. Other journalers write a story after a brief dialogue with their drawings. Still others write a story days or weeks after a drawing is finished, because they need time to mull it over. We are confident that each of you will find your own best way to work with your imagery.

The journal drawing *Blue Ball/Orange Cat* (Figure 5-5) was done by Christina. She began a dialogue with her images by asking the big blue ball one question: "What would you like to say to me?" The ball responded, "I am wound up so tight it makes me a dense, dark ball. If I uncoiled and spread out, I could let in the light. I am deep at the core—there are leaves weighing on me, filling the space so I cannot uncoil, let in the light, breathe or expand. Make room so I can uncoil, so that soul can permeate and open me up even more."

When Christina brought her drawing into group, she read the response she received from the ball, knowing that it symbolized her own inability

Figure 5-5. **Blue Ball/Orange Cat,** *from the journal of Christina*

to relax and let go of worry and fear. The message was clear—she needed to unwind herself so that she could let in the light of trust and understanding that would open her up to her soul's voice. After she explained to the group what she believed her drawing meant, someone pointed out a form that looked like an orange cat stretching out its paw. Christina had not seen this form at the time she created it. Later, returning home, she could not get it out of her mind. What did it mean? she wondered. This prompted a poem.

I am wild
feline
walking the stalking walk
step by step in the moonlight.
Footfalls without sound
just one shoulder then the other
dips and rises again.
Scent of a shadow
stirs a primal memory.
Nonchalant eyes watch
intent
patient.

She revels in the sunlight
watching her shadow
feeling the power and sinew
she can run and jump
climb, fight
slink almost slither
play and catch
strike fear into others
then, walk away, uninterested and bored.
Watching herself
sitting regally like the sphinx
full of questions
and secret answers.

This poem revealed to Christina the inherent power of her imagery. She is the cat, with the innate ability to run, jump, climb and strike fear into others. Although she is full of questions, she also holds the secret answers.

Christina is a cancer survivor, and like all survivors of life-threatening illnesses, she lives with the endless fear of recurrence. Fighting that fear, opening up to life and embracing all that it has to offer, is the greatest challenge a cancer survivor faces on a day-to-day basis. This drawing and the poem it inspired were not about ordinary fears and uptight attitudes. For Christina it was about trusting in her own power to take charge of her life, even though her shadow is a constant companion.

When Kate Siekierski first drew *Blame vs. Curiosity, Wonder, Awareness and Awe* (Figure 5-6), she felt agitated. The paper seemed too small to adequately express what she felt, but she decided to make it work anyway. "The drawing began," she said, "with a piece of earth in the center. As I started to work with the drawing, I felt a sense of expansion inside myself, so much so that the size of the drawing didn't matter anymore.

"At first, the moonlike figure reminded me of a muskrat, but the more I looked at it, the more it felt like an otter. I was so joyful that it was an otter, because I was aware that in Jamie Sam's *Medicine Cards*, otter represents the feminine, the elements of earth and water.

"When I finished the drawing, I asked otter what it was trying to say to me. This is the answer I got: 'Freeness of love without jealousy. The finer qualities of woman need to be strived for in both men and women, so that a unity of spirit can be achieved.' Then I asked otter what it wanted me to do. It said, 'Stop your addiction to worry. Become otter and move gently into the river of life. Flow with the waters of the universe. Discover the power of woman. Drop the seriousness and learn to play, so that fear can roll off your back.'"

After Kate finished the dialogue with her otter, she wrote the following story:

Figure 5-6. **Blame vs. Curiosity, Wonder, Awareness and Awe,** *from the journal of Kate Siekierski*

One morning as otter was taking her usual morning swim, she noticed how quiet the world had become. She swam from shore to shore and saw how serious human beings had become. They did their chores and went off to work with these blank looks in their eyes and heavy hearts. Otter was so sad, she began to sob and sob and sob. Other otters came and comforted her and shared her sorrow.

As this went on, a little creature, who at first scared them because they thought he might be a demon in disguise, asked if he could help. With some trepidation they agreed, since trust seemed important *at the moment. He told otter that he could help her temporarily grow to a size beyond the earth so she could hold it and send some new energies to help the people on earth reawaken to their playful spirits. Even though there was some suspicion, otter agreed. She looked into the creature's eyes, and as she did, she felt this incredible love, and then she grew and grew and grew. It's amazing how love can make the littlest being feel big. When she grew to a size big enough so that she could embrace the world with all her heart, she felt the meeting of the masculine and feminine. She could then see people begin to soften. They stopped moving so seriously and began to throw their heads back and laugh.*

Otter beckoned the help of snake, as this was a huge task for one otter alone. Snake came to watch and support. The negative energy came oozing out in fire form, and people who walked on the earth began to live their lives with more intuition, passion and less rigidity.

And so this is the story of how one being got involved in helping the creatures who walk the earth to live life with more joy, love and creativity. Otter wondered what the world would be like if all creatures opened their hearts and looked into one another's eyes without judgment, full of warmth and love and passion.

Through this story, Kate discovered how to do what otter advised in her dialoguing session. To become otter, Kate must learn to balance her own feminine, loving and accepting nature with her inner masculine drive to walk through the world with a serious focus on work and achievement, which she grew up believing was necessary in order to succeed and survive. What Kate learned from this story is that true success and

survival can happen only if she refocuses her energy and begins to see the world from a broader perspective. Doing so will allow the love in her heart to grow and grow until it affects all those around her.

It is truly amazing to see how a simple story can encapsulate our issues, while at the same time presenting a means to resolve them through the gentle guidance of the heart rather than the head.

Since we like to practice what we preach, we authors both keep our own visual journals right along with our group participants. For the last two years, Susan has been struggling with the fear of separation from her parents as they move into the final stages of old age. In group, she shared a story inspired by a journal drawing entitled *A Family of Three* (Figure 5-7).

Susan told us what her intention had been when she began the drawing. "I wanted to come to a place of peace with my own situation as an only child caring for two aging parents. I am very close to them, and there is a great deal of confusion over the reversed role of caretaker having to make decisions for them. At the same time, I am dealing with my own anticipatory grieving as I prepare for their eventual departure from this earth plane." Then she read her story.

There once was a family of three who moved through the landscape of life with ease, curiosity and a sense of adventure. One day on the road, they encountered a tree in their path. They asked it to move out of the way. To their astonishment, it asked, "What for?" Then the tree began to grow horns and ears. They asked the tree for it's name and why it showed such disrespect for their journey. The tree replied, "My name is Sam—Sam the Man Tree." Sam explained

Figure 5-7. **A Family of Three,** *from the journal of Susan Fox*

that moving from their path would be difficult, for his roots were firmly planted in the earth. The path was very narrow, so the family of three pondered their plight.

Soon the sky opened up and a pink cloud towered above the tree. A wise, gentle force then beckoned them to split up, saying, "Go round the tree, one at a time, or two on one side and one on the other." A simple solution, yet one of concern. The tree was BIG! Each wondered if they would get lost or fall off the trail or ever be able to meet again on the other side of the tree. The tree listened to the family's concerns and spoke. "The choice is simple: either stay where you are or find the courage to separate for a while and continue your great adventure together later."

The family of three always believed in going forward, in taking risks, in never playing it safe. So their decision—to move forward, two on one side and one on the other, with the hope of meeting again on the other side—reflected their need to be on their way no matter what the risk. A big, rooted obstacle in the path is always an opportunity to find the courage to be true to one's beliefs.

When she finished reading, Susan explained the message. "The story reminds me that it is difficult to know which way to go when separation seems imminent. But even when faced with an insurmountable obstacle in my path, it tells me that I must go forward. I know now that this obstacle is my fear. If I move past it, I will come out on the other side and meet my parents again—but only if I uphold the family tradition of taking risks and moving forward. If I remain stuck in fear, the life they gave me will have been wasted."

By now we hope you have discovered

through your own experiences as well as those of our group members that when we learn to hear the messages from our images, we connect with the sacred place beyond conscious thoughts and fears. This ancient source of knowledge taps deep into the root of our core selves. We call it the dwelling of the soul, the wellspring of divine inspiration. You may call it whatever you wish.

We feel certain that there is not a person on this planet who has not at some time been in touch with this source. All too often, however, whether through mistrust, disbelief or ignorance, we get disconnected and are unable to sense the guidance that is always there. Fortunately, our images can reconnect us.

CHAPTER SIX

Art from the Heart

Since taking this visual-journaling workshop for almost two years now, I have come to realize that not everything can or needs be figured out by the brain. Expressing one's self through imagery has a way of accessing deep-seated emotional information and moving it through the body, creating an awareness of one's inner being that the mind alone cannot achieve. At first, I didn't think I could even draw or paint, but I soon discovered, like everyone else in this group, that I can. And now I'm hooked.

—**Joan Dwyer**

Every year since we first began offering our visual-journaling workshops, our journalers have put together at a local gallery an exhibition called Art from the Heart. Their collective goal is to choose journal drawings, or paintings, collages and three-dimensional constructions inspired by their journal work that represent the profound insights they have experienced as visual journalers. Accompanying each selection is a written statement that reflects the journaler's thoughts about the piece.

To give you a taste of what it would be like to attend an Art from the Heart exhibition, we decided to dedicate this chapter to a color section featuring journal art that is similar in nature to the kind of work you might see in our annual show. Of course, all of the journal work displayed in this book is art from the heart. A color section, however, offers us an opportunity to display pieces that must be seen in color to be fully appreciated. In addition, we also tried to select work that best illustrates the kind of heart-touching revelations our journalers have come to appreciate and expect from their work. Each selection is accompanied by a written statement that explains what the journaler learned while doing that particular piece.

The journal images and statements that follow are windows to the inner worlds of their creators. The workshop participants who share their stories here feel their experiences were valuable not only to themselves but to others. Only by sharing our innermost thoughts and fears as well as our deepest hopes and dreams can we give others the courage to express what their hearts need to say.

Figure 6-1. **Catpower,** *from the journal of Joan Dwyer*

"This piece emerged out of a need to find a symbol that represented a new definition of my own sense of empowerment and personal identity. It is a collage with a leopard leaping through a small opening in a net. As I fitted the pieces together, I could feel the power in the image becoming real. But it still needed more, so I drew a large pink heart and glued the cat form to it. This was important to my new identity, because I wanted to be sure that everything I do comes from my heart. The difference now is that the cat image means that my heart and my power are connected.

"This piece still hangs in my office eighteen months after I created it. It is a reminder that I am no longer caged, a reminder of my power. The cat springs forward from nature and from my heart, leaping out of confinement and boundaries. Shortly after I created this picture I started my own business."

Figure 6-2 (top). Sketch for **Fire in the Dark,** *from the journal of Ishmira Kathleen Thoma*

"In this journal exercise, I began with a quick, loose sketch that became the inspiration for a more developed illustration that I later completed. This piece I called **Fire in the Dark.**"

Figure 6-3 (bottom). **Fire in the Dark,** *Ishmira Kathleen Thoma*

"My intention, as I began working with the journal drawing above and then with this fully developed illustration, was to express the changes I felt coming from my heart, changes that encompassed an increase of compassion for myself and others. The woman in the drawing is giving birth to her heart, symbolized by the Grail. The light coming from that chalice-like form represents my new sense of expanded consciousness and joy."

Figure 6-4. **Spirit Woman,** *from the journal of Birgitta Grimm*

"When I first did this drawing, I had no idea what it was about. The image just came to me. Two weeks later, I found out that a friend had died on the very day I drew it. That's when I understood what the drawing represented—it was an image of her spirit passing on." A while later, after thinking about her death and what it meant, the drawing of her spirit passing inspired this poem:

A light shines brightly, showing her the way,
releasing her from the pain of death.
Tears come to her as she is lost in her beloved's eyes.
Her soul envelops her closely,
love surrounding and supporting her
as she passes through the narrow space.
She dreams of the softness of her mother's womb
cradling her with quiet warmth.
Water swirling and caressing her as
she swims with the creatures of the sea.
Floating, dancing, filled with love,
protected as only they can be when

encircled by the power of the heavens.
The spirits all around her
as she arises from the hurt,
sheltered amongst the forgotten ones.
Guided by their wisdom
as she flies towards the light,
soaring with her heart held between her arms.
She emerges with ease and dignity
towards the timeless space,
always embracing her loved ones,
at no time forgotten and never far away.

Figure 6-5. **Untitled,** *from the journal of Linda Hill-Wall*

"When I first created this piece, my mind judged it as pure junk, so it was headed for the trash. Then someone suggested that I continue to work with it, to play with it, to cut it up and see what happens. Reluctantly I did. Out came the X-Acto knife, and for some reason I also took out assorted dishes, cups and other house-hold items. Not knowing what I might do, I just started to play, using a cup and then a small saucer to trace shapes with the knife until I had collected a pile of shapes. As I continued to play with these shapes, I became energized and strangely invested in the process. I was lost in the feeling of play; it became a sort of prayer, a whole new way of being, with no agenda, no control, no judgment.

"The finished piece tells me to step into the unknown, step into the land where there is no judgment, where nothing is without value. Let go of the illusion of control—step into the dark, the rich, the unexpected. Trust, listen, grow."

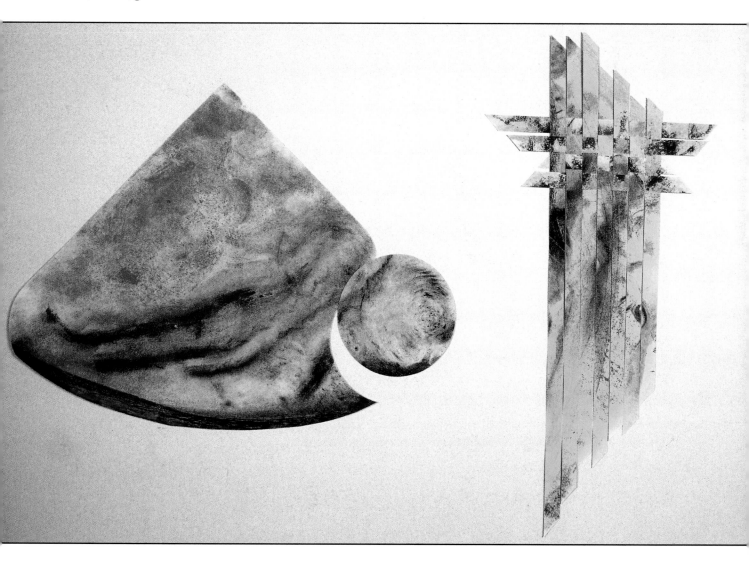

Figure 6-6a. **Superman,** *from the journal of Rob Blais*

"While I was working on these two drawings, I didn't know what they represented until after they were finished. First I did the one on the left, in which I drew an image of myself looking lighthearted, lying on the grass alongside the train. Then I crossed over in my journal to the right page and continued to draw the train. That's when the whole feeling of the picture started to change.

Figure 6-6b. **Superman,** *from the journal of Rob Blais*

"When I finished the second drawing and looked at both of them, I realized they represent the two sides of myself. One side is very easygoing, enjoying life, while the other is like a high-speed train—always going somewhere fast. I want to get off the train and be that relaxed person, but the voices in my head, the critics who preach the work ethic and the importance of money and getting ahead, won't let me. This drawing enabled me to finally hear my own voice—the voice that is willing to take a risk to get back to being the person I want to be."

Figure 6-7. **Cross,** *from the journal of Sabra*

"This drawing represents my inner struggle, that constant feeling that says, 'Yes, you can! No, you can't!' The red rings around my neck constrict me. They create a blockage around my heart, which is holding down the intersection of my true beliefs with the universe, not allowing them to interact. The gold cross represents my true beliefs. The blue heart feels heavy. It cannot get past the red blockage. The green is my soul essence, and it is just existing—waiting. I need to transform this feeling by changing these images."

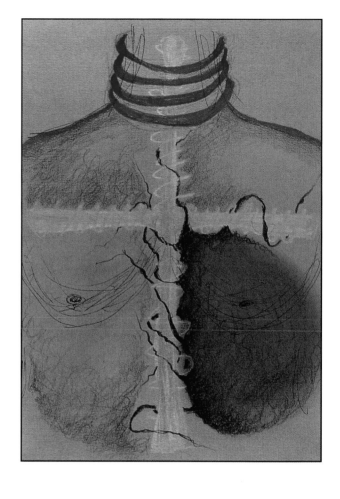

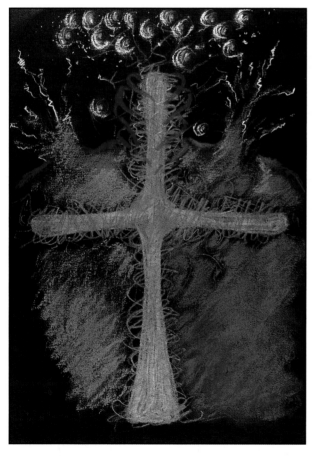

Figure 6-8. **Cross Transformation,** *from the journal of Sabra*

"This second drawing is the transformation image. The cross vibrates so intensely that it breaks the red rings and dissolves the blockage, allowing a connection to my core beliefs that tell me, 'I can do anything! There is true abundance in the universe!' I am not religious, so the cross image was a surprise, but it broke through and left openings for my heart and soul to interact completely with the universe."

Figure 6-9. **Heart & Soul,** *from the journal of Cherie*

"With this journal drawing, I felt like I got to see my soul, and I learned that my passions are intense. The colors flow into each other. There are dark parts, but even they show the intensity of my passions. The drawing feels grounded, yet the energy is moving and wants to experience how all things in life work."

Figure 6-10. **Universe,** *Kate Siekierski*

"My intention is to stop the busyness, the mind chatter and little housekeeping tasks that consume my time. I want to be in touch with love, to open my heart. When I am limited and bounded by negativity, I dislike my life, my job feels stupid, my marriage feels unhappy, my cats are too needy, my friends don't like me, I'm old and unattractive, my family doesn't care—basically, life sucks. Negativity sucks out life.

"Doing this piece, which started out as a journal drawing and turned into a collage, connected me to my sense of fun. The colors of the circles felt like my chakras spinning. I had a feeling of ambivalence about putting in the color green, but when I did, it felt good. Putting in the stars, the planets and the mystical stickers was incredibly fun. I felt blissed out. I felt childlike. This journal piece, filled with star people, is my universe. With it, I am connected."

Figure 6-11. **Woman on Fire,** *a series of two, from the journal of Kerri Brennan*

"This drawing shows me that the sun is within me and my center is strong. Everything will work out."

Figure 6-12.

"With this drawing, I quiet my mind."

Figure 6-13. **The Ant,** *Cherie*

"My intention as I began this journal drawing was to draw the landscape of my heart, and in doing so, to experience my heart without judgment and to hold it with love.

"Upon completing the drawing, the landscape told me that my heart is an exciting place to be—it is lush and flowery with an abundance of color and vegetation. The ant is part of my life. It reminds me that my heart is connected to the outside world. The ant is industrious, an independent explorer and yet community oriented, just like me. The lushness of this landscape of my heart makes me want to cry because it is so beautiful. It makes me feel sad to have questioned my heart for so many years when it is perfect just the way it is! I often forget that my heart and I are one."

Figure 6-14. **Colored Pencil Woman,** *from the journal of Donna DiGiuseppe*

"My intention with this drawing was to get rid of the nervous tension in the back of my neck and in my stomach.

*"A person close to me was in a raging tizzy. Although I try not to get involved in his stuff, I tend to absorb the discomfort and it has a physical effect on me. This drawing gave me an outlet. It gave my stress a place to go— a home. The reds and purples represent my confusion. I had all this **stuff** in me that wanted to come out. As I worked on the drawing, I felt more connected to myself, to both my negative and positive energies. Eventually, my frenetic energy changed to blues and greens, which calmed me, and the yellow-oranges gave me strength.*

"The figure that emerged from the drawing is me. My energy is coming out of my body, neck and head. Looking at my legs, I can see that one is weak and the other is strong. There is a whirlwind of circular energy coming out of my body. The orange Xs are decorations like medals of honor or high antennas pulling me up and reminding me of my strength and intelligence. I am standing on a path with rocks, weeds, and grass, which make me feel in harmony with the environment.

"I realize now that the message in this drawing is to honor my potential, anchor myself more, and believe that I have all I need inside of me."

Figure 6-15. **Soul Bowl,** *from the journal of Clare Sartori-Stein*

"I was working with collage materials in an attempt to express an image of my soul. I knew I needed to make a container to hold it. As I worked to shape this bowl from seed pods, dried grasses, delicate gold string, glitter, feathers and soft cotton, slathering layer upon layer of light, delicate paper, I was intently working on both the inside and outside of the bowl at the same time.

"As I worked on the outside of the form, a feather emerged from the cotton. It reminded me of a verse: 'I am a feather on the breath of the Great Spirit. I soar with the joy of serving.' That's when I realized that this bowl symbolized my soul's purpose—to serve others. The bowl is the cup or chalice that I offer to others. Knowing this, I am in awe of the greater mystery yet to come."

Figure 6-16. **Woman Planting Seeds,** *from the journal of Mary Sargent Sanger*

"For over forty years I have been seeing myself through someone else's shame. I wanted to change that image of myself, but the size of my journal was too limiting. I began to work with a large piece of paper, applying finger paints and then squeezing the paper. As I did, this powerful form emerged, exposing my playful, creative self. I am now dedicated to developing my creative process. This piece seemed grounded with all the earth colors, and the form—the being—was reaching her arm out to drop seeds on the earth. I love to plant, and once I realized that my reality was not shaped by someone else's opinion, I began to plant new seeds of hope."

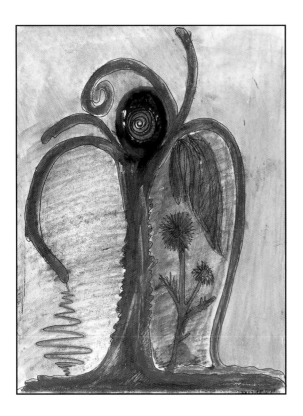

Figure 6-17. **Life, Death & Transformation,**
from the journal of Birgitta Grimm

*"I did this drawing in an effort to make some
sense of the sadness and confusion I was feeling
after the sudden death of my brother-in-law,
and the pain I was also feeling at the same time
because I had to leave my home and my mother
in Sweden. The branches of this tree go every
which way, seeking a home. One branch points
upward to the heavens while the other points to
the ground with some kind of energy spiraling
out of it into the earth. The center of the tree
feels like an abyss spinning, and so bleak, empty
and heavy that I added the flowers for hope. The
leaves protect it and the ground is solid."*

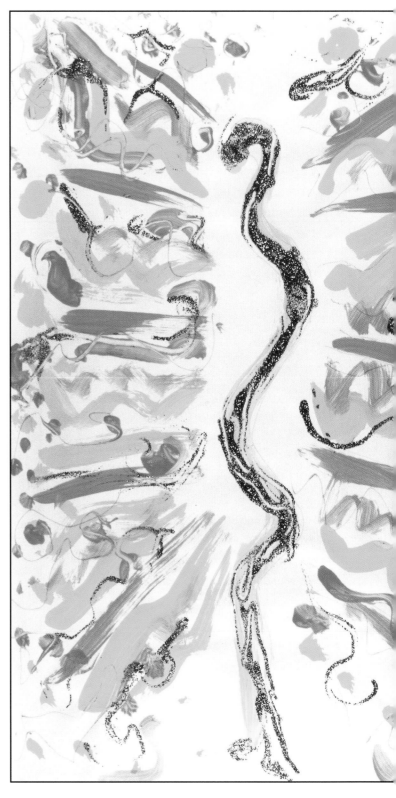

Figure 6-18. **The Swizzle Stick,** *from the journal of Jeannine Gendron*

*"I asked this drawing, 'Who are you?' It answered, 'I am a swizzle
stick, transformed. I was a part of you, the part that was repressed,
the part that is in hiding. There is still something hiding. Will you
come out?'"*

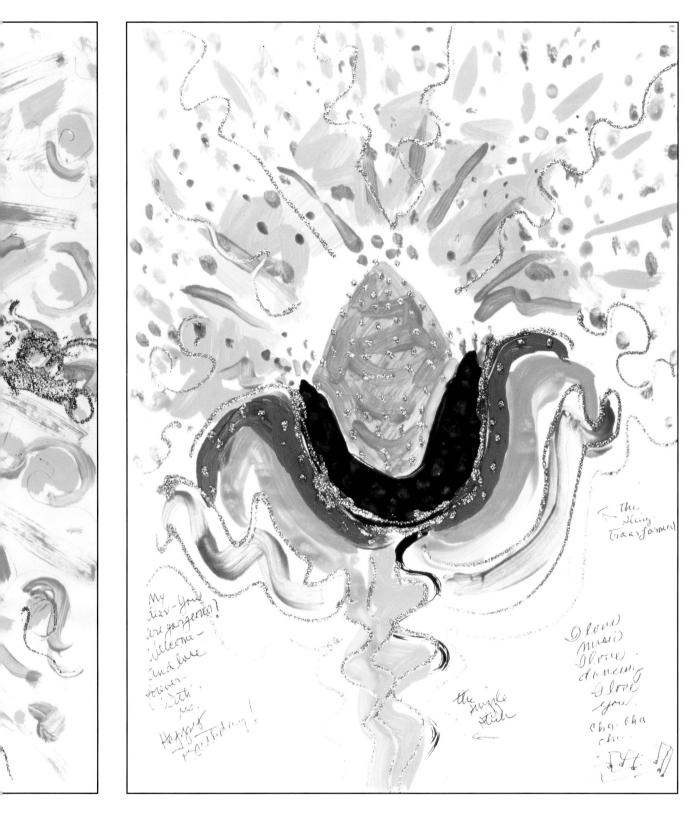

Figure 6-19. **My dear, you are gorgeous!,** *from the journal of Jeannine Gendron*

"I did a second swizzle-stick drawing. It says, 'My dear, you are gorgeous!'"

Figure 6-20. **Being of Light,** *from the journal of Kate Siekierski*

"As I write about this drawing, I know the image is me, a being of light, star-shaped, stretched out, feeling big, full of myself. There is a diamond-shaped door that is my center. The diamond always reminds me of something a boss wrote on a drawing of mine when we were in a workshop together over twenty years ago. 'Kate, you are a gem—a real diamond.' As I write, I feel the love that this woman had for me. My inner critic wants to sabotage me right now as it says, 'She felt bad for you because you had Hodgkin's disease.' My compassionate side says, 'That's not true.' I go back to the diamond door. I feel something open within me, my hands fill with energy. I realize it is a door to aliveness. It's a door to knowing—knowing what I need, which is movement, dance and massage, but mostly to sit quietly."

CHAPTER SEVEN

Overcoming Fear

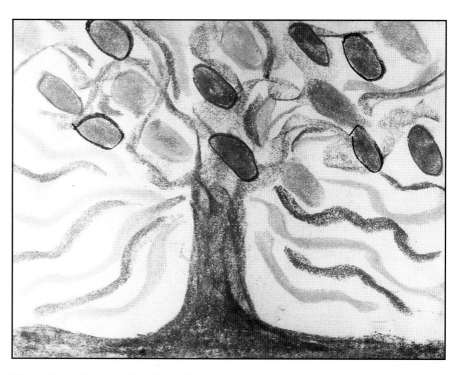

Figure 7-1. **The Guk Tree Transformed,** *from the journal of Ishmira Kathleen Thoma*

"As we throw away the arrows and the spears, a freeing of our energy occurs. As we let go of judgment and fear, everything becomes infused with the soft light of compassion. We feel how, in response to fear, we have boxed ourselves in. The expansive peace comes in as the rigid harshness flows out. We can breath again. Flaws disappear into what simply is. Acceptance and a floating sensation come into the belly—a release."

hen Ishmira Kathleen Thoma drew *The Guk Tree Transformed* (Figure 7-1), she discovered one of the most important lessons of fear: If it can be seen from a different perspective in which judgment is suspended and compassion embraced, fear can be transformed into fertile ground from which peace, expansiveness and acceptance grow. The quote accompanying her drawing came from a dialoguing session she did with her images. It reflects her desire to throw away the arrows and spears of judgment so that she can release her own "rigid harshness" and accept what is. The message she received from this drawing became a turning point in her life.

Ishmira had been struggling for seven years, since the birth of her daughter, with the same issue that so many young mothers face—that they will not be good mothers if they devote time and energy to the pursuit of a career. Ishmira is an artist and professional graphic designer who also teaches classes in a healing-art technique called spontaneous painting.

Refusing to be imprisoned and immobilized by a fear that she no longer wished to carry,

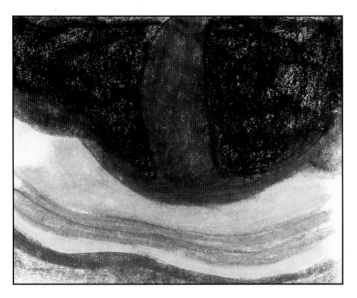

Figure 7-2. **The Guk Tree,** *from the journal of Ishmira Kathleen Thoma*

Ishmira began, through a series of journal drawings, to expunge it from her life. The first drawing in that series was called *The Guk Tree* (Figure 7-2). The second drawing she titled *Judgment* (Figure 7-3) and the final drawing was *The Guk Tree Transformed* (Figure 7-1).

    The Guk Tree expressed how this fear felt inside her body. Upon completing the drawing, she wrote the following passage in her journal: "My creativity, represented by the green ground and the rainbow colors beneath it, is stifled, pushed down by this barren, lifeless tree, which is surrounded by all the dark, horrible guk in life. Where is this guk coming from, this notion that I can't be a good mother and an artist at the same time?"

    To answer that question, Ishmira drew *Judgment* (Figure 7-3), an image of herself curled up with an arm covering her head to protect herself from the onslaught of spears and arrows.

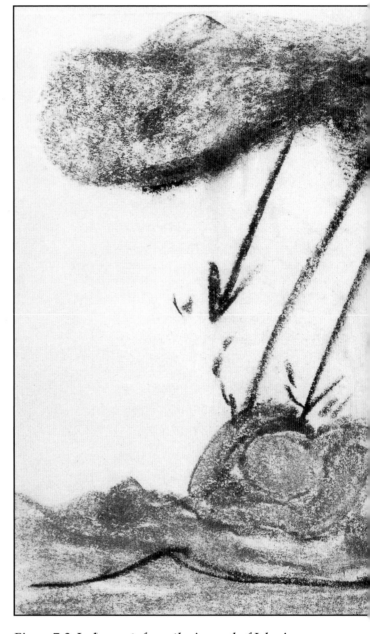

Figure 7-3. **Judgment,** *from the journal of Ishmira Kathleen Thoma*

These she identified as the judgment of others, particularly her mother, who, in her youth, had denied her own creative drive to concentrate on raising her children. "This judgment from my family really hurts," she told the journaling group

my artwork. I need that in my life, too. It is a hard balance to achieve."

After Ishmira explained to the group what her drawing of judgment was about, we asked her if she knew what emotions this fear set off. She told us that several years ago she had started a drawing that she was never able to complete because it left her feeling so angry and filled with despair. The following week she brought this drawing into group. We have included it here, even though it was not drawn as part of a visual-journaling exercise, because it demonstrates how important it is to not only identify our fear, but also the emotions it generates.

Ishmira told the group that this drawing, which she called *Old Judgment* (Figure 7-4), helped her identify what she had felt for years. "The woman in this drawing," she said, "represents judgment. I am the figure curled up on the ground. One of my wings, which symbolize my creativity, has just been severed by judgment's sword. The reason I could never finish this drawing was because it brought to the surface all my feelings of anger and despair. So when you asked what emotions were set off by my fear, I remembered this old drawing. Until I did these three journal drawings, I could never get past my anger.

"What's really interesting to me," she continued, "was how I came upon the healing image of *The Guk Tree Transformed.* Something told me to turn the first drawing of *The Guk Tree* upside down so that I could literally look at my fear from a different perspective. That's when I realized that with the rainbow on top, the guk surrounding this ugly tree—my anger, my despair, the

as she talked about her drawings. "This is where the fear comes from, the feeling that I will never be able to live up to my family's ideal of a good mother. As for myself, I love my daughter and I want to be with her all the time, but I also love

Figure 7-4. **Old Judgment,** *Ishmira Kathleen Thoma*

judgment—was fertilizer. All this could become the fertile ground from which my creativity could grow and flourish. That thought, that vision, gave birth to *The Guk Tree Transformed* and enabled me to let go of my fear and anger.

"It amazes me to think how I allowed myself to remain captive to this fear for so many years. But no more. I have found a way to compromise, to work it out with my husband so that I can have time do my artwork and still give my best to my little girl. It doesn't have to be either/or. That's my family's belief, not mine. I can't change the way they think, which is what I wanted to do all these years, but I can change the way *I* think. I don't have to be shackled to their values, either in action or in thought."

DISCOVERING THE LESSONS OF FEAR

Like Ishmira, we all have fears. When we are attached to an unreasonable or unrealistic

fear, the soul, speaking through the body's sensations, cries out for change. If we fail to hear its cry, the body responds with messages of anger, resentment and hostility. We can become immobilized by our fears, allowing them to limit our decisions and choices, or we can use them as motivators to discover the life-altering lessons they have to impart. Our fears can teach us how to separate ourselves from the beliefs and expectations of others and form new beliefs that are more compatible with what we need to fulfill our personal destiny. As always, the choice is up to us.

As Ishmira discovered, as soon as we decide to confront fear by questioning its validity or relevance to our lives, exploring its source, and asking what lessons it has to teach, it can become the stepping stone to our highest potential.

WEEK FOUR

Overcoming Your Fears

To overcome fear you must first recognize that it exists. Then you need to access and release the emotions it generates. Release opens the pathway of communication to your soul. Through the voice of your soul, you discover the lessons your fear has to teach you.

For this fourth week of visual journaling, you will have an opportunity to look at all of your fears. Then you can determine which ones are unrealistic or unreasonable and have limited your dreams, goals and desires. Finally, you can decide which of these fears you are ready to release and transform from limitations to stepping stones to greater possibilities.

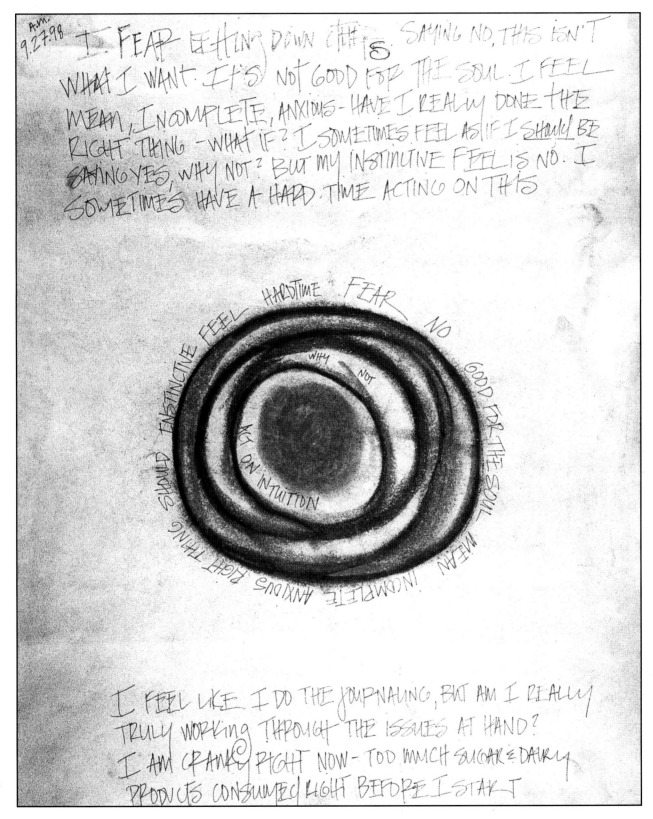

A.m.
9.27.98
I FEAR LETTING DOWN OTHERS, SAYING NO, THIS ISN'T WHAT I WANT. IT'S NOT GOOD FOR THE SOUL. I FEEL MEAN, INCOMPLETE, ANXIOUS - HAVE I REALLY DONE THE RIGHT THING - WHAT IF? I SOMETIMES FEEL AS IF I SHOULD BE SAYING YES, WHY NOT? BUT MY INSTINCTIVE FEEL IS NO. I SOMETIMES HAVE A HARD TIME ACTING ON THIS

I FEEL LIKE I DO THE JOURNALING, BUT AM I REALLY TRULY WORKING THROUGH THE ISSUES AT HAND? I AM CRANKY RIGHT NOW - TOO MUCH SUGAR & DAIRY PRODUCTS CONSUMED RIGHT BEFORE I START

Figure 7-5. **I Fear Letting Others Down,** *from the journal of Bre Churchill*

EXERCISE #1

Discovering Your Fears

The following exercise will help you identify your fears. On a journal page, write down any of the fears listed below that are present in your life, even though you may not experience them on a daily basis.

- Saying yes
- Saying no
- Letting others down
- Making mistakes
- Failing at a new endeavor
- Succeeding at a new endeavor
- Making a decision
- Changing my mind
- Changing careers
- Changing jobs
- Losing my job
- Having too little money
- Having too much money
- Being homeless
- Retiring
- Being unable to take care of myself

- Being alone
- Living alone
- Sleeping alone
- Children growing up and leaving home
- Children dying
- Children getting hurt
- Loved ones dying
- Loved ones getting hurt
- Having to care for an aging parent or relative
- Placing a loved one in a nursing home
- Natural disasters (hurricanes, earthquakes and so on)
- War
- Endings
- Leaving a relationship
- Starting a new relationship
- Intimacy
- Commitment
- Marriage
- Divorce
- Becoming a parent
- Making friends

EXERCISE #2

Identifying Unreasonable or Unrealistic Fears

Once you have identified your fears, you can sort out which ones are unreasonable or unrealistic.

How can you tell the difference? Some fears

are essential to our survival, such as the fear of rape, mugging, break-in, war or natural disaster. Then there are fears that are a natural and instinctive part of life, like losing a loved one, losing your job or failing at a new endeavor. None of these fears are unreasonable or unrealistic,

- Rejection
- Feeling left out
- Losing a close friend
- Using the phone
- My own death
- Chronic illness
- Life-threatening illness
- Telling others that I have an illness
- Recurrence of a life-threatening illness
- Having a relapse from an addiction
- Admitting that I have an addiction
- Getting treatment for an addiction
- Gaining weight
- Losing weight
- Getting too thin
- Accidents
- Rape, mugging, physical assault
- Having my home broken into
- Asserting myself
- Being interviewed
- Speaking in public
- Entering a room full of strangers

- Change of any kind
- Doing something that appears stupid or foolish
- Stating my opinion when others disagree
- Standing up for my beliefs
- Buying a house
- Driving
- Feeling helpless or incompetent
- Being taken advantage of
- Disapproval of others
- Feeling vulnerable
- Being criticized
- Being seen as a loser
- Admitting that I am wrong
- Apologizing
- Getting angry, depressed or violent
- Admitting that I am happy
- Admitting that I am unhappy
- Feeling as though I am not good enough
- Feeling undeserving
- Feeling as though I am not smart enough
- Any other fears not included in this list

unless—and this is the important qualifier—they control your life and/or cause you to behave in a way that limits you or others.

Ask yourself this question as you look at each fear you wrote in your journal: Does this interfere with my life or someone else's life in any way? If your answer is yes or maybe, then underline it. Then go through the list again and place a check mark next to any fear that you feel ready to eliminate.

Figure 7-6. **Umbrella Woman,** *from the journal of Kerri Brennan*

"With my eyes closed, I was breathing deeply and thinking of fear. I saw an image of rain and an umbrella and a frightened little girl holding the umbrella. My fear, I realized, was creating furniture to sell—more specifically a fear of failure. I thought about this. Let's say I paint recycled furniture and try to sell it. What if no one buys it? Does this mean I am a failure? That's an opinion. If I look at it differently, then I can see that trying something I enjoy and having an opportunity to grow and learn in the process certainly isn't failing. It all depends on how I decide to look at it. When I look at my fear differently, the scared little girl becomes beautiful and powerful, a fairy with enough light for everyone. I have clearly worked through most of my fear in this drawing—without realizing it. The message is that to never live is to fail. Not achieving what you set out to do doesn't mean you have achieved nothing."

WHAT TO DO IF YOU FIND YOURSELF STUCK IN A PAINFUL EMOTIONAL EXPERIENCE

As we mentioned in the beginning of the book, visual journaling can bring up painful feelings that you may not always be prepared to handle. If you find yourself upset by the emotions that surface during this six-week program, you may want to see a professional counselor or therapist. A counselor can aid you in processing overwhelming or particularly intense emotions by helping you see things from a different perspective, and will provide support and validation if you feel confused or unsafe.

A REMINDER TO CONTINUE YOUR REGULAR CHECK-INS

Although you are using this week to identify and explore your fears, we would like you to do at least one or two regular check-in exercises in your journal as well. No matter what the weekly focus is, throughout this six-week program and beyond, it is always important to check in so that you stay in touch with how you feel about the events and circumstances of your day-to-day life.

EXERCISES TO HELP YOU ELIMINATE FEAR

The four journal exercises in this chapter have been designed to enable you to eliminate unrealistic or unreasonable fears from your life. Keep in mind, however, that overcoming fear does not mean you will never feel its pull again; it simply means that you have decided that it will no longer control your thoughts, choices and behaviors.

In the first exercise, you select a fear that you feel ready to work with, and access an image that best expresses what it feels like inside your body.

When you have completed your drawing, you can use the self-exploration questions that follow to learn what your drawing is trying to communicate to you.

The second exercise helps you access any emotions connected to your fear. Drawing your emotions and exploring their relationship to your fear helps you release its emotional hold on you. In the third exercise, you ask your soul for an image that represents what this fear is meant to teach you. In the fourth exercise, you destroy the image as a symbol of your intention to eliminate this fear from your life.

You can perform the series with each fear on your list. However, because this is extremely important, life-altering work, we suggest that you not process more than two fears in a single week. The exercises can be emotionally exhausting, and they can also dredge up unhealed emotional wounds that may take time to sort through before you are completely ready to release them. Once this six-week program has ended, you will still have plenty of time to work through your list of fears.

EXERCISE #3

Accessing an Image of Your Fear

Now that you have identified your unreasonable fears and have checked off those you wish to eliminate, select one to work with in this exercise. (You can work on as many fears as you like, but only one at a time.) Open your journal to the next two side-by-side blank pages and write that fear on top of the left-hand page. Beneath it, write a sentence or two explaining why this fear is either unrealistic or unreasonable. Then write your intention for the drawing, which should in some way reflect your desire to access an image of what this fear feels like inside your body. Now get yourself into a comfortable position and follow the directions in the guided visualization that follows. Feel free to use movement or sound.

- Close your eyes and take several deep breaths. Pay attention to the rise and fall of your chest as you breathe in and out. Continue doing this until you feel connected to your body.
- Focus your awareness on your fear. Try to remember the last time you felt it. What was going on? Allow that experience to replay before your mind's eye. Let yourself feel the sensation of that fear. Notice where it is located in your body.
- Focus your awareness on the place or places where you are experiencing the physical manifestation of your fear. Imagine what it would look like if it were an image.

- When you have an image or idea, open your eyes and draw it on the opposite journal page.

Self-Exploration Questions

When your drawing is complete, you will have a graphic representation of your fear. Look at this image for a while. Use the left-hand journal page to write the answers to the self-exploration questions. These questions can help you learn more about what your drawing is trying to communicate to you.

1. What does your drawing tell you about the way you experience this fear?
2. What do the colors tell you?
3. Have you experienced this fear lately? If so, what were the circumstances?
4. Look at each image, shape, color or symbol in your drawing. If they could speak, what would they tell you about your fear?
5. Does this drawing give you any indication of what you need to do to overcome your fear?
6. At what other times in your life have you experienced this fear?
7. As you look at your drawing now, do you see any special message or meaning around the general issue of fear? If so, what is it?
8. How do you feel about your reactions to this fear?
9. Would you like to change how you react? In what way?

Figure 7-7. **Fear,** *from the journal of Christina*

"My fear is that I can't handle it—classes, school, programming, my psychology course. I'm afraid I'll make the wrong choices and decisions. I'm afraid I won't be able to support myself. I'm afraid I'm wrong!"

10. What could you add to this drawing or take out that would reflect the change you want to make? Once you know what your drawing needs, go ahead and change it.

11. How do you feel about your altered drawing?

12. What does this altered image tell you about your fear?

Figure 7-8. **Out or In,** *from the journal of Joan Dwyer*

"Out or in—in or out. Does the box serve me any longer? Do I need to be put in my place? I could be in or out—both are fun—without being confined. The box served a purpose—a purpose of survival growing up. I am bigger than the box. That box contains so many parts. I give all aspects of myself freedom to emerge and dance—the jester, clown, cat, woman, dancer, snake, jaguar. Lord, assist us all to move forward to free ourselves of old shackles and move into your light."

EVERYONE'S IMAGE OF FEAR IS DIFFERENT

Although fear is an emotion we all share, no two people experience the same fear in exactly the same way, nor will their images of that fear be the same. The next few journal drawings demonstrate the wide variety of imagistic expressions our journalers create when they attempt to identify and overcome their fears.

Figure 7-9. **Fear is . . . ,** *from the journal of Kate Siekierski*

"*Fear is . . . failure, hopeless, little, powerless, angry, rageful, suicidal, out of control, weepy, sorrowful, overwhelmed, unhappy, hurt, not heard, demanding, exhausted, tired.*

"*I have been aware of my hands today. I want to smash things, hit things, punch. I played my drum outside and did some screaming. It was somewhat soothing. Then I drew a black cave with a little yellow being inside. This picture is the transformation of it. After drawing the black cave with the yellow being, I made handprints all over the paper. One of the handprints I ripped out and put inside the cave where it could support the little yellow being. This is to remind me to be gentle and soft with myself when I'm feeling all of this.*"

Figure 7-10. **Animal Mask,** *from the journal of Donna DiGiuseppe*

"*As I drew on flat paper with the intention of learning about the fear I feel of leaving my father's energy, a black pencil figure quickly formed. It appeared to be throwing up. My inner organs are red. There are black charcoal walls squeezing in on me and my head is whirling. The piece of small cotton wipey that I used to smudge the charcoal had marks and colors on it. I spent time touching and folding it, as if it were my security blanket. Then I folded the paper to fit in my hand. That was important, because everything needed to be squeezed and shut tight—shut off from the outer world. Then I needed fire. I took a candle, lit it outside and began burning the flat edges. I rubbed the embers into the soil, and then I squeezed the paper into a ball, gently rubbing the paper on the earth, asking for release from my father's energy. I came inside, opened the paper, and a wolf mask appeared.*"

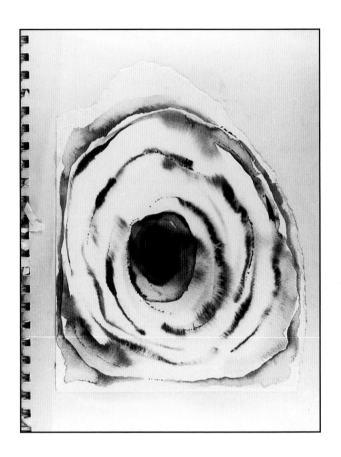

Figure 7-11. **The Fear That I Am Alone,** *from the journal of Sabra*

"The fear that I am alone—that all the beautiful things in the world are not for me. The dreams I have about doing art, finding a great place, will not happen to me—good stuff happens to others, not me. Talking to the picture. . . . The center is me. I'm lost in this well of deep despair—I'm separated from the world, and things in life need to be complete. The grayness swirls around me and won't let me out, won't let me pass through it. I don't believe in myself—if I believed, I could get out of this despair. What do I need to get out? Wings of hope to fly past it all, to be carried away. Very strong wings. I need to be carried away, but I need the strength of the universe to get me there. I need to believe and have hope."

BELIEVING IN YOURSELF TO OVERCOME YOUR FEARS

Like Sabra, we all need to believe and have hope that we can overcome our fears. But it is not enough to merely transform the image of your fear; you must also believe in your ability to enact the transformation. Consequently, change always begins with the decision to believe in yourself. To do this, you must understand that your inability to believe in yourself came from years of hearing others tell you that, like Sabra, you were not good enough, not special enough and that good things happen only to others. These beliefs do not have to be your beliefs. Transformation begins when you make the choice to reject negative and

destructive beliefs. Then and only then can the transformed image of your fear be activated from within.

Sabra drew her transformational image of wings (Figure 7-12). When she brought this drawing into the journaling group, she said, "When I drew these wings, I didn't want to glue them down. That told me that the key to overcoming fear is to take action, to not be stuck in place. At this point in my life, the real sadness comes from thinking that someone said all these things to me—that I was undeserving and that good things wouldn't happen for me. I am ready to leave those beliefs behind. They don't belong to me anymore. I am ready to fly."

Figure 7-12. **Wings,** *from the journal of Sabra*

EXERCISE #4

Asking Your Soul What Your Fear Has to Teach You

Fear, like all experience, comes into our lives to teach us what we need to know in order to become the person we were born to be. To realize our full potential, we must be able to take on all the challenges that life presents. Fear is often the only obstacle that prevents us from tackling those challenges. While we may blame our obstacles or limitations on lack of money, opportunity, ability or the unwillingness of others to cooperate, in truth it is our own unwillingness to face our fear that gives power to these conditions. When we refuse to be limited by our fears, everything begins to change—the way we think, the way we act, and the way others see us.

Change begins with one thought alone: *I will not let this stop me.* This thought becomes the trigger that enables us to move forward. However, we need fuel to keep us moving. That fuel is supplied by the knowledge we gain when we learn the lesson of our fear. That lesson is one that only the soul can provide. This next exercise enables you to ask your soul for a symbol that represents what your fear has to teach you. Once you know the answer, you can use your fear as fuel to move ahead with confidence and assurance.

When you are ready, open your journal to the next two blank side-by-side pages, and write your intention on the left-hand page. Your intention should clearly state your desire for a symbol that represents the lesson you are meant to learn. Now, get yourself into a comfortable position and follow the directions.

- Close your eyes and take several deep breaths. Focus on your physical body by tuning into the rise and fall of your chest. Continue doing this until you feel connected to your body.
- Imagine that your conscious awareness is a tiny bead of light nestled deep within your heart center. The heart is the keeper and dwelling place of the soul. With your attention focused on your heart, reflect on the image of the fear you expressed in your previous drawing.
- As you see this image with your inner eye, ask your soul to replace it with a symbol of what this fear is meant to teach you.
- When you know what the symbol is, open your eyes and draw it in your journal.

Figure 7-13. **This Is My Sword,** *from the journal of Donna DiGiuseppe*

"I have discovered an area where my hand wraps around the paper like a sword handle. Everything is coming up all at once—tears, anger, pain, hatred, guilt, power. When I hold my sword, it empowers me to slash, to kill, to be the best swordsman. No one can touch me. People fear me. It's a psychic death. I want to kill the energy between my mother and me. There was so much fire. So much heat, growling, animalistic battle. Lions fighting. Two female lions, fierce, biting, hitting. Tears of hurt. I have been dancing with my sword and sounding out growls. Now I feel calm, as if something passed through. The skin on my left hand has gotten very itchy—a sign of release. I want to release my mother's energy in a kind way. I want to apologize—Mom, I'm so sorry for whatever I put you through. I did not mean it. I was confused and lost. I'm not blaming myself for the circumstances or the interactions and dynamics. As an adult I want to say I am sorry so that I can move on without this blockage, burden and judgment. I condemned myself at the time to be a horrid person who would never marry—no one would ever love me because I was ugly. I told myself that I was not like the other girls and they would never like me. I distanced myself in a big way. And now I see I really distanced myself from myself, disowned myself, and took on the image of my mother, never wanting to be anything like her. Yet I am probably all of her. My sword has helped me cut through time, pent-up feelings and emotions. I love my sword. I love my mother. I love myself."

SELF-EXPLORATION QUESTIONS

When you have completed your symbol drawing, take some time to look it. When you are ready, go back to the left-hand page of your journal and write your responses to these questions.

1. How does this symbol make you feel?
2. What do you sense it is trying to tell you about your fear?
3. What do the colors mean to you?
4. What are they trying to tell you?
5. If your symbol could speak, what would it say about the lesson you need to learn?
6. How can you use this lesson to change your previous beliefs?
7. How can you use your new beliefs to move past your fear?
8. How can your fear become an asset?
9. When you overcome your fear, how will your life change? Be specific.

EXERCISE #5

Releasing Fear from Your Life—Burning Ritual

Now that you have described how your life will change, you must go through the final step—releasing this fear from your life. If you are ready, and most importantly, *willing*, you will release your fear by burning your drawing. This ritual activates your intention to release your fear on the conscious, subconscious and cellular levels, which, as you recall from our explanation in Chapter Four, are the three levels on which change must take place.

When you are completely certain that you are ready and willing to release this fear, you may continue.

• Remove the drawing of your fear image from your journal and take it outside to a safe and private place where there is no wind. You will also need a pack of matches or a lighter and a small bottle of water. Find a place where the ground is free of all combustible debris. Make a circle of stones large enough to surround the drawing. Place the drawing inside the circle and repeat the following affirmation out loud:

> *I am ready and willing to release this fear from my life. Now that I have learned the lesson of my fear, I no longer need to carry it with me. I will never allow this fear to interfere with my life again.*

• Close your eyes for a moment, take a deep breath, and ask the universe, the Spirit that moves through all things, Divine Guidance, God or your higher self—whatever you are most comfortable with—to witness and acknowledge the release of your fear.
• Open your eyes and set your drawing on fire. Watch it burn, bid it good-bye. As the

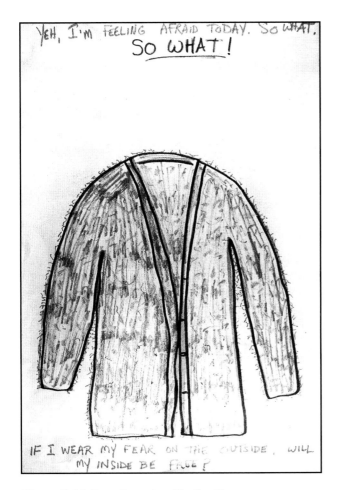

Figure 7-14. **Fear Sweater,** *Sheila Charron*

"Slimy green is my fear color. Recently I was attracted to this ugly, hairy sweater, the color of my fear. After much deliberation, I bought it. When I wear the sweater, I say, "Yeah, I'm afraid! So what?" With this sweater, my shoulders go back, and I get this attitude. I'm letting you know this is my fear sweater, and when I'm scared to death, putting it on lets me take the fear that I feel on the inside and wear it on the outside. And somehow that makes it all better."

last remnants disintegrate, thank your fear for all that it has taught you.

• When there is nothing but ashes left, cover them completely with dirt or pour water on them so that they cannot reignite.

What We Fear Will Reappear

We subscribe to the belief that what we fear will reappear. In other words, if we worry about a particular fear and allow it to control our lives, we will eventually draw to ourselves the very thing we fear. This belief is based on the ancient universal law of attraction. In modern times, Albert Einstein proved that light behaves as a particle if the observer expects it to. However, if the observer expects light to behave as a wave, it behaves like a wave. If the most minute elements of our subatomic universe can be influenced by our thoughts, then it is prudent to assume that all matter and all events can be controlled to some extent by human expectations.

In other words, what we expect is what we get. For example, if a man fears losing his job, he will begin to unconsciously act in a negative and counterproductive way that eventually jeopardizes his job. On the other hand, if the same man not only recognizes his fear but also decides to change the beliefs that created it, then he will begin to consciously alter his behavior in a positive and constructive way, consequently transforming the fear into an asset.

We hope you will continue to repeat the exercises in this chapter until you have worked through all the fears you are ready to release. Be aware, however, that there may be fears you are not prepared to explore and release right now. This is perfectly all right. It is important to honor your own resistances, since they might indicate that you have not yet learned the lessons of your fear. When the time is right to release it, you will know. Confronting fear may well be an ongoing process throughout your life.

Figure 8-1. **One Eye Open, One Eye Closed,** *from the journal of Kerri Brennan*

"For years I tried so hard to be perfect, to take care of others and to not be vulnerable. My life was a struggle of wanting others to accept me as I really was and accepting myself. I didn't want to show myself to the world because I didn't believe in myself. This drawing helped me understand that if I look only at the outer world, I will never see who I am on the inside. But if I keep one eye open to look outward at others and one eye closed to look inward at myself, I will be in balance. When I am in balance, there is no struggle. I can open up and let my inner light shine. And when I do, I want to reach out and share it with others—to let them see the real me."

CHAPTER EIGHT

Resolving Inner Conflict Through Soul Wisdom

The activity of making art is therapeutic, for it enables me to reconcile and express polar feelings and ideas.

—Richard Newman

Kerri Brennan kept herself closed off from others for most of her life because she was scared—scared to let herself and others see who she really was on the inside (Figure 8-1). The only part of herself she dared to reveal was her outer shell of perfection, which she carefully controlled to protect her inner vulnerabilities.

Kerri did what we all do early in life in order to accommodate the expectations of family and culture—she adapted. She ignored who she was on the inside and became instead the person she thought she had to be so that she would fit in, be loved and accepted. Kerri believed that if she were perfect, if she took care of everyone else, then no one would ever see her fears or her needs, no one would ever disappoint her, nor would she disappoint others. But eventually living with this kind of inner conflict became too great a struggle. Kerri's inner self, the voice of her soul, spoke out through her visual-journaling imagery. It showed her the way to find balance between her need to live harmoniously with others and accept and honor herself exactly as she was without the outer facade of perfection.

Although it may manifest differently for each of us, we all experience inner conflict at some time in our lives. For many of us the attempt to reconcile the differences between what we feel and how we act is a lifelong struggle.

How Inner Conflict Arises

Inner conflict occurs when we feel one thing and then say or do another. It is directly related to a belief system that tells us that our own ideas and opinions are untrustworthy and that we must defer to the opinions of others. Carried to the extreme, we can eventually find it nearly impossible to make independent decisions about our lives.

BECOMING AWARE OF INNER CONFLICT

Our inner conflicts become apparent when we catch ourselves saying yes when we want to say no, being dishonest about what we really feel and attempting to please others at the expense of our own needs. Inner conflict involves what Richard Newman described in this chapter's opening quote as *polar feelings*—feelings that are diametric opposites.

An example of polar feelings might be a situation in which you feel extremely angry at something your spouse or partner did, but instead of telling them, you convince yourself that it doesn't matter, it's not worth getting upset over, and you act as if nothing happened. Or perhaps you are at a party and someone tells a racist joke. You see red inside, but instead of leaving or speaking up, you laugh along with everyone else.

The common defense most people use for this kind of oppositional behavior is usually expressed as clichés: "You gotta go along to get along," "Don't make waves," or "Laugh and the world laughs with you; cry and you cry alone." But we prefer to line up on the side of psychologist and best-selling author Wayne Dyer, who often says that as long as we are attached to other people's opinions of who we are, what we do and what we think, we will never know true freedom. Each time we violate our own beliefs, opinions and needs in order to be accepted by others, we extinguish a small piece of our soul. Eventually that soul flame becomes nothing but a smoldering ember.

HOW FEAR DRIVES OUR INNER CONFLICTS

Fear is the fuel that drives our inner conflicts. At the core of all our conflicting thoughts, behaviors and actions is the ingrained belief that if we fail to meet the expectations of others, we will suffer their disapproval, condemnation and the withdrawal of their love. That is why Kerri

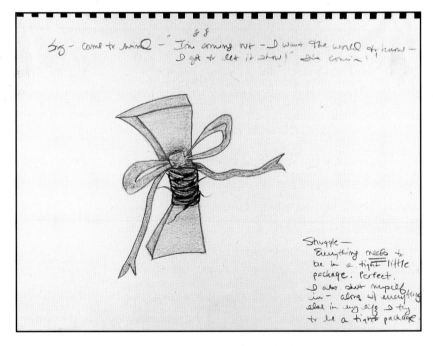

Figure 8-2. **I'm Coming Out,** *from the journal of Kerri Brennan*

"Always needing to be a tight little perfect package, just to fit in, ties me up, restrains me. As I drew this wrapped-up package being squeezed to death, I felt the lyrics of the song 'I'm Coming Out' playing in my head. And that is what I'm doing. No more perfect packages, because I'm coming out!"

was scared. Revealing her true self was, in her mind, dangerous, until she finally recognized that the real danger was in *not* being the unique individual she was born to be.

As you learn to recognize and question your fears—particularly those based on erroneous beliefs—you get better and better at seeing the source of inner conflict when it comes up. The work you did in the previous chapter, in which you identified your fears and the life lessons behind them, lays the groundwork that will help you see the correlation between your unreasonable fears and the inner conflict you experience when they are triggered.

What Causes Inner Conflict?

Inner conflict is caused by a discrepancy between your thoughts and your feelings. More specifically, your mind and its belief systems, which use judgment and critical thinking as a measuring stick to evaluate whether something is good or bad, right or wrong, tell you what you *should* do, what you *should* think, and what you *should* feel. At the same time your soul, which uses divine guidance as its measuring stick, is trying to tell you through your body's feelings and emotions what it *knows* is best for you, based on your ultimate life purpose and the path you are meant to walk in order to fulfill it.

Inner Conflict Is a Primary Source of Stress

When your head and soul are in conflict, your body responds by feeling stressed. Remem-

Figure 8-3. **The Light within Me Bursting Through,** *from the journal of Kerri Brennan*

"In this drawing, I did come out as I drew the package wrappings transforming into a dress, wings sprouting and the light within me bursting through the ribbon bodice. Before, I had allowed myself to be shut in. Now I can feel the light within me coming forward."

ber all those signs of stress we pointed out in Chapter Four—tight muscles, increased blood pressure, the release of stress-producing hor–mones—that compromise the immune system and cause massive headaches, backaches, neck pain, sleeplessness, fatigue and an inability to

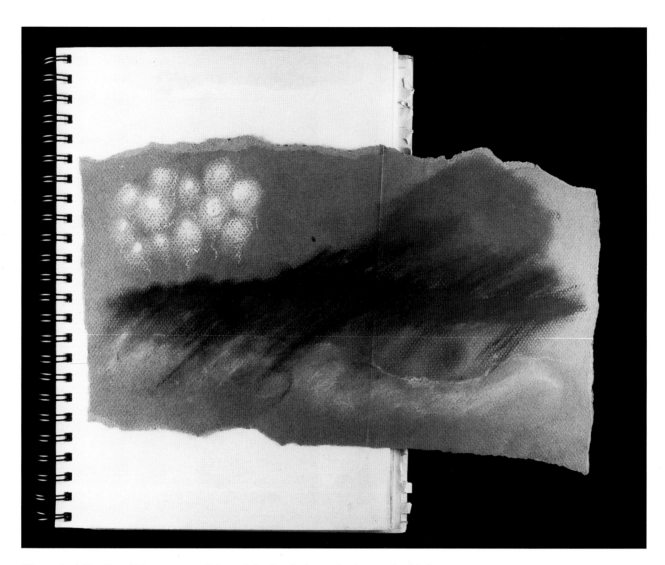

Figure 8-4. **Feeling Disconnected from My Soul,** *from the journal of Sabra*

"As a little girl, I had lots of energy, which was not acceptable to my family. It was too much for them. Gradually I stopped my passion for life. I was given fear as a replacement—the fear of being too much, the fear of not being loved if I was not doing the right thing, and the fear of my passion. My passion caused me pain.

"I still feel this conflict. It disconnects me from my soul. To express it, I needed to get this image on paper in my journal. Blue is my soul/spirit, green is my heart, the yellow dot in the corner is a hole in my heart. Red is the separation, criticism, the negativity, the anger of not being healed. I also want to move from where I am living and change my job.

"The red radiates into my soul and heart and vibrates so loud that they cannot connect. White is light; the little light beings in the upper left corner are dancing the voice of the universe to me. They do not interfere because they know this is my journey, but they do try to speak. But can I ever hear them over the vibration of criticism and negativity that separates me from my soul?"

concentrate? When you find yourself experiencing any of these warning signs, you can bet you are smack in the middle of a king-sized conflict between your head and soul. If you fail to pay attention, not only will you jeopardize your freedom to be your true self, but eventually your body will pay the price for a lifetime of unresolved inner conflict.

WEEK FIVE

Resolving Your Inner Conflicts

To resolve an inner conflict, you must first recognize that one exists. The best way to detect an inner conflict is to pay attention when a particular area of your body feels tension, discomfort or pain, such as a headache, a migraine, irritable bowel syndrome, nausea or acid stomach. Any of these may be a sign of conflict-related stress. Then take a look at what is going on in your life at the time you feel these symptoms. Are you speaking or acting in opposition to what you feel emotionally? If so, then you need to examine the issue at hand. Of course, there is no better way to explore the many sides of an issue and its accompanying emotions than with visual journaling.

The exercises for your fifth week of visual journaling are designed to help you look at any issue in your life that may be creating a conflict between your thoughts and feelings. In the first exercise, in order to explore the polar feelings that create the conflict, you will compare your thoughts about the issue to the images that represent your emotional reaction to it. Then you

will use imagery to give voice to your soul's perspective. Through this exercise, you will come to appreciate the soul's ability to see beyond the judgments and expectations of the mind and the wisdom inherent in its directives.

There is a final exercise that enables you envision a symbol that represents your soul's purpose in this lifetime. Knowing this purpose enables you to stay attuned to your inner guidance when you are faced with conflicting choices in the future.

ISSUES THAT CREATE INNER CONFLICT

Sometimes inner conflict involves only small things, like whether or not you should go with a friend to a movie when you would rather stay at home, or whether you should graciously accept Mom's moth-eaten drapes for the new paladin window, or honestly tell her, "No, thank you." You tell yourself that these matters are too trivial to risk hurting someone's feelings. You chastise and criticize yourself for being self-centered as you agree to minor concessions that deep down leave you feeling resentful and at odds with yourself. At other times you may lie and pretend to have other plans when a friend or relative invites you out, or you may keep telling Mom that you love her drapes, but you just haven't had time to put them up.

Unfortunately, inner conflict is not always limited to life's small concerns. Most of the conflicts that we suffer through are more like Kerri's. They involve disharmony between how we perceive ourselves and how we want to be perceived by others. Inner conflict also arises

Figure 8-5. **Clutching at My Time,** *from the journal of Sabra*

"I am clutching at my time to keep it to myself—I feel guilty—I feel distorted by the guilt. What is so wrong with wanting time to myself—time to do what I want, be who I want? No, I should be calling so-and-so. I should be spending time with my mother. I should be doing more at my job. Why can't it be about me? Because it would be selfish?"

Figure 8-6. **Floating on the Cloud of Knowing,** *from the journal of Sabra*

"Knowing who I can give time to will be a growing experience for me—knowing what I need to spend time doing and what I just do not need to waste my time on. The blue cloud represents knowing and growing in a safe, guilt-free atmosphere where I have plenty of time for all. I need to grow."

when we feel guilty about what we need and want in order to be happy and fulfilled, and what others demand from us so that their needs are met. The next journal drawing, also by Sabra, is a perfect example of exactly how this kind of guilt can provoke the torment of inner conflict.

To resolve her feelings of guilt, Sabra did a transformation journal drawing, which she called *Floating on the Cloud of Knowing* (Figure 8-6). After completing this drawing, she wrote some responses to it on the left-hand page of her journal. Those responses appear next to the drawing.

After allowing some additional time to reflect on both the drawing and her responses, Sabra wrote the following comments on the back of her drawing: "My growing makes the world a little better for everyone—I do not need to make everyone better. The violet blue in this drawing is my life as I want it to be. It is the centering, the belief that it can happen. I deserve it! I am worthy!"

Like Sabra, we all must learn to believe that we are worthy and deserve time to pursue our own interests, to have our needs met, and to enjoy lives that are rich, full and abundant in every way. Until we learn this soul lesson, we will always be in conflict as we continue to put others' needs ahead of our own. As Sabra so aptly put it, "I don't need to make everyone better. My growing makes the world a little better for everyone." Our job on this planet is to make the world a little better for everyone by being the best we can be. We will never do that if we do not allow ourselves the time and space to grow, learn and accomplish everything for which divine intention has brought us into this lifetime.

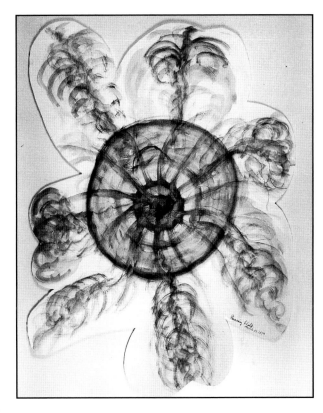

Figure 8-7. **My Growing Soul,** *from the journal of Bob Morse*

"For so long I have been like a prisoner because I felt that I did not deserve to be loved by anyone, and most importantly, by myself. I believed that I could get this love only from outside if I earned it. I set out to find another way to live that was not always about struggle. As I learned to journal with images, the practice of staying in the moment, being open and accessing the places in my body that held years of pain, helped the walls come down. I began to see that what was inside me was beautiful. I began to feel more deeply, and through this was able to manifest an image that represented myself. This drawing is me in process—it is my soul growing."

The struggle to reconcile our own needs and what others need can tear us apart. This is especially true when we are forced to deal with such life-altering events as marriage and divorce, the death of loved ones, leaving a job, accepting a job, moving away, aging and illness, as well as questions that arise over money, relationships, raising children and career-path decisions. These are the big concerns in life, the mind bogglers, the heart wrenchers. What we choose to do about them can change forever our own lives and the lives of those around us.

EXERCISE #1

Identifying the Sources of Inner Conflict in Your Life

This is a two-part exercise to help you identify and clarify what causes conflict between your thoughts and feelings around a specific issue. In Part One you name the issue and describe your verbal thoughts about it—the shoulds, woulds and coulds that run through your mind. These thoughts will help you determine whether you have erroneous beliefs that keep you attached to unreasonable expectations that may be in direct conflict with your feelings, needs and desires. In Part Two, you use body-centered awareness and visualization to access an image that expresses your feelings about this issue, independent of your thoughts.

Part One

- Open your journal to the next two side-by-side blank pages and write down a few words that describe an issue that causes you inner conflict.
- Close your eyes for a moment. Allow yourself to think about this issue, then open your eyes and write down each of the following sentence stems. Beneath each one, write as quickly as possible as many endings to each sentence stem as you can think of:

1. When it comes to this issue, I think I should . . .
2. When it comes to this issue, I think I shouldn't . . .
3. When it comes to this issue, I would like to . . .
4. When it comes to this issue, I do not want to . . .
5. When I think about this issue, I feel . . .
6. Every time this issue comes up, I'm convinced that other people think I . . .
7. What I really want to happen with this issue is . . .
8. If I had my way with this issue, I would . . .
9. If I were honest with others as to how I really feel about this issue, they would think that . . .
10. If I were really honest with myself as to how I feel about this issue, I would know that . . .
11. The best solution I can think of when it comes to this issue is . . .

- Next, answer this question:

As you look back over the endings you wrote for the sentence stems, do you notice any negative thought patterns, self-incriminating tendencies or attachments to other people's opinions? If so, what are they?

Any negative thoughts, critical tendencies and attachments to other people's opinions that you identify are most likely the main reasons you have been conflicted about this issue. As you move on to the second part of the exercise, you compare what you have just learned about your thoughts with what you will learn about your feelings. This helps you determine the nature of your inner conflict.

Part Two

Part Two involves the use of body-centered awareness and guided visualization.

To begin, write down your intention for your next drawing, which should reflect your desire to access an image of what this conflict feels like inside your body. Then get into a comfortable position and follow the directions in the guided visualization. As always, feel free to use movement or sound.

- Close your eyes and take several deep breaths. Pay attention to the rise and fall of your chest as you breathe in and out. Continue doing this until you feel completely connected to your body.
- Now focus your awareness on the conflict that you identified in Part One. Try to remember the last time you experienced this conflict. Allow the episode to replay before your mind's eye. As you do, let yourself feel the physical sensations that accompanied it. Notice where in your body you feel this conflict.

- Allow your conscious awareness to move into the places in your body where you feel the physical manifestation of this conflict in the form of tension, stress, discomfort or pain. Now imagine what this feeling would look like if it were an image.
- When you know what it would look like, open your eyes and draw it on the next blank journal page.

Self-Exploration Questions

The image in your drawing is a graphic representation of how you feel about this issue. Look at your image for a while, and when you are ready, use the next blank page to write your responses to the self-exploration questions. If you compare your responses to the sentence endings you wrote in Part One, you will understand the difference between your thoughts and your feelings surrounding this issue. That difference in viewpoints is exactly what causes you to feel conflicted.

1. What does this drawing tell you about your feelings over this conflict?
2. What do the colors tell you?
3. Have you been experiencing this feeling of conflict recently? If so, what circumstances provoked it?
4. Look at each image, shape, color and symbol in your drawing. If each one could speak, what would it tell you about your conflicted feelings?
5. Does the drawing give you any clues or ideas about how to resolve this conflict?

Figure 8-8. **Expressing My Conflicting Values,** *from the journal of Bre Churchill*

"This drawing expresses my struggle with the issue of having money and fine-quality things, yet being in tune with the environment. I want to create abundance for myself, have a new car and possibly own my own business. How do I start when my values are in conflict?"

6. At what other times in your life have you experienced the same inner conflict?

7. As you look at your drawing now, does it convey any special message or meaning about your conflict? If so, what?

8. When you compare your responses to these questions with your sentence endings in Part One, can you identify the difference between what you think and what you feel? How does that difference create conflict? Write down the differences. It may help to create two columns, one labeled "My thoughts about this issue," and the other, "My feelings about this issue."

EXERCISE #2

Understanding Your Soul's Resolution of the Conflict

Knowing what causes your inner conflict—the discrepancy between thoughts and feelings—does not necessarily resolve it. To do that, you may need the kind of guidance that only your soul can provide. This exercise helps you tap into the wisdom of your soul. As you connect with it, you will come to appreciate the soul's ability to see beyond the judgments and expectations of the thinking mind into the deeper meaning of an issue. When you see an issue through the eyes of the soul, you can understand the wisdom inherent in its directives.

In the next guided visualization, you move your awareness into your heart center, the keeper of the soul. From within your heart, you will ask your soul for a symbol that represents a resolution of this conflict, one that is in the best spiritual interests of not only yourself but of other involved parties as well.

When you are ready, turn once again to the next two side-by-side blank pages in your journal. Write down your intention to access a symbol that represents your soul's resolution of this conflict. Next, get into a comfortable position and follow the directions in the guided visualization. As always, use movement or sound if you like.

- Close your eyes and take several deep breaths. Pay close attention to the rise and fall of your chest as you breathe in and out. Continue doing this until you feel completely connected to your body.
- Now imagine that you have the power to move your awareness to any part of your body. With that idea in mind, allow your awareness to drift gently toward your heart center.
- When you sense that your awareness is there and that you are fully present to your heart, ask your soul for a symbol that represents a resolution to this conflict that is in the best interests of all concerned.
- When you know what this symbol is, open your eyes and draw it.

Self-Exploration Questions

The symbol in this drawing represents your soul's resolution of the issue. Look at this symbol for a while, and then when you are ready, use the next blank page to write your responses to the self-exploration questions.

1. What do you feel the symbol represents?
2. What does it have to do with your inner conflict?
3. What is your soul trying to tell you through this symbol?
4. Look at the colors you used. If each one could speak, what would it say to you about your conflict?
5. Has this symbol ever come up for you at any other time in your life? In what context?
6. If you answered yes to the previous question, is there a connection between the appearance of this symbol now and its appearance in the past?
7. If your symbol could speak, what would it say to you?
8. After answering these questions, what do you feel is your soul's solution to this conflict?

USING THESE EXERCISES TO RESOLVE OTHER INNER CONFLICTS

These exercises provide a tool that you can use whenever conflict arises in the future. We also recommend that you spend some time thinking about unresolved conflicts from the past that may still be affecting you unconsciously. If you come across memories that provoke tension between your thoughts and feelings, work through them with visual journaling. Remember, old issues do not heal on their own. They simply fester beneath the surface like a low-grade infection, just waiting for a new conflict to appear. Then they flare up all over again and spread their toxins into every area of your life.

Figure 8-9. **Verbal Criticism Can Be Psychic and Spiritual Annihilation,** *from the journal of Kate Siekierski*

"A source of conflict occurs at work when I hear others making judgments. Sometimes I join in and then feel guilty later. Sometimes I'm quiet and get a holier-than-thou attitude—I'm better than them. At other times it doesn't matter what others say or do, although it's hard to sustain that position.

"Judgment is about energy loss. I feel like this sack trying to protect itself, and all these little pellets or beebees are being fired at me. This drawing makes me think of the rhyme, 'Sticks and stones may break my bones, but names can never hurt me.' Not true! Words can be piercing. They go right through you. They make you lose form. I get anxious when I'm around critical people. I get anxious when I'm critical. Judgment puts someone up and someone down—I'm OK, you're not.

"This feeling of conflict begins to transform as I draw the blue lines. They feel soothing. There is a path. I feel energy pulsing in my feet and hands as I imagine blue, compassionate energy. The center figure in the drawing starts to take on the shape of a heart. Once we connect to our hearts, the energy starts to pulse."

TRUSTING YOUR SOUL'S SOLUTION TO YOUR INNER CONFLICT

The most difficult part of receiving a symbol that represents your soul's solution to your inner conflict is learning to trust it. When we do this exercise in our journaling groups, many participants tell us that the soul's way of resolving inner conflict was not at all what they expected. Their minds, which had been filled with judgment, blame and criticism, often wanted to resolve issues through retaliation or intimidation—a real "I'll show you!" kind of attitude. But their souls' symbols represented resolutions that were gentle, kind, loving and forgiving. Some attitude adjustment was required in order for them to bring themselves around to this radically different point of view.

To follow their souls' guidance, our journalers had to let go of pride, the need to be right and fear about how others might perceive them. But when they did let go, every one of them told us that they found a sense of peace and contentment. Furthermore, when they began to actually implement their souls' resolution, something remarkable happened. The anger and resentment they had carried for so long seemed to melt away. Then, to their amazement, everyone else involved in the conflict seemed to change attitudes and behaviors, even before our journalers had an opportunity to speak with them. Was this mere coincidence? Not at all! When we change, everyone around us changes as well, and not a word needs to be spoken.

Figure 8-10. **Mother Turtle/Turtle Heart,** *from the journal of Brenda Bullinger*

"This drawing began to take shape as the center green image reminded me of both a turtle and a heart. Mother Turtle, to me, suggests wisdom. The heart is also wisdom—the wisdom of my soul coming through it. I am always drawn to heart shapes and always conscious of trying to hear my heart and soul so that I can follow their directives. I am learning to respect this inner wisdom, especially when I am up against challenge or adversity, even when it goes against the tide of my mind's opinions. Before, I thought heart and mind were separate, but now when I'm connected to my images, I experience a universal sense of knowing. Through that knowing, my heart and mind can agree. It is not the finished product that touches me with visual journaling, it is the messages I receive through the process."

Emotional change produces an energetic change. Energy, quantum physics has proven, is the life force of our physical bodies. Quantum physics has also demonstrated that our energy fields are not confined to our physical bodies, but connect to the energy fields of all other living things. Thoughts are also energy waves; thus our thoughts travel through our energy fields and interact with other people's energy fields. That is how we exchange unspoken information. Remember the last time you stood in a supermarket line and just knew, without a word being said, that your checker felt hostile and angry? Have you ever walked into a room and known, without a smile or gesture exchanged, that a particular person found you attractive or interesting? We have all had those experiences. We call it picking up someone's vibes. And that is exactly what we are doing—picking up energy in the form of thought vibrations. So the next time you are tempted to think nasty thoughts about another person, you may want to reconsider.

Our soul's wisdom is always available to guide us through every issue, conflict, choice and decision of our lives. The problem is that most of us are so preoccupied trying to get what we want out of a situation that the voice of our soul goes unheard and unheeded. The next chapter shows you how to expand your visual-journaling practice into a lifelong endeavor that will keep you connected to your soul's inner wisdom and guidance.

CHAPTER NINE

Expanding Your Visual-Journaling Experience

The natural language of the soul is the image, and through the discovery of our own unique forms we can find access to an inner guidance that is truly remarkable.

—Douglas Gilbert

We hope that the first five weeks of this visual-journaling program have helped you to take care of some of your own unfinished emotional business, just as it did for Claire Sartori-Stein, whose work is shown in Figure 9-1. Like all of our workshop participants, you too have had an opportunity to learn how to use your body-mind's language of imagery to go deeper into your emotional experiences than words could ever take you. In the process, you have learned how to express the voice of your soul through your journal artwork. But there is still so much more that you can do with visual journaling.

What you have learned from this book so far only scratches the surface. If you continue to use visual journaling on a regular basis, you will uncover things about yourself, your feelings, your desires and your aspirations that might otherwise

Figure 9-1. **Moon Beings,** *from the journal of Claire Sartori-Stein*

"I entered the visual-journaling class with the goal of taking care of any unfinished emotional business, and at the same time assisting myself in discovering who I am, as well as what my purpose in the world might be. Through this work I came to a deep appreciation for the power of the visual-journaling process: it affirms the wisdom inherent in my being, which patiently awaits its access through the door of imagery."

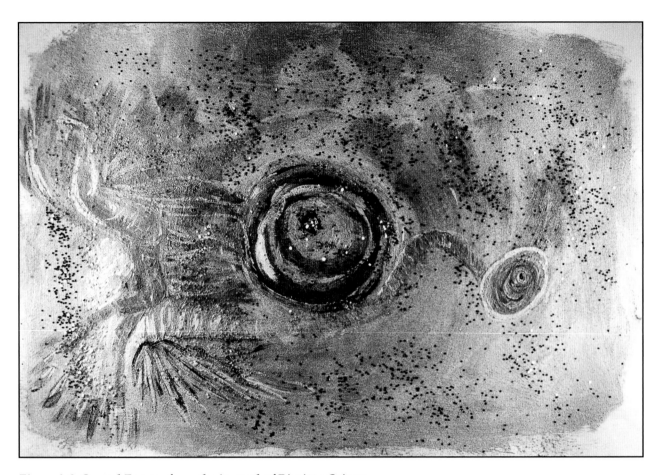

Figure 9-2. **Sacred Forms,** *from the journal of Birgitta Grimm*

"Since I began doing visual journaling more than three years ago, I notice so much more of the world around me. I not only see myself differently, I see others differently as well. I have an acceptance of others that was not there before. My relationships have improved. I listen more attentively without trying to change people. And I have come to accept my own need to create art that I was reluctant to acknowledge before. I can feel my creativity in my heart. When I make something, no matter how small, I can feel my heart expand.

    "In this drawing, to find my own sacred forms, a woman appears and writes this with her nondominant hand: 'She rides faceless bringing light. She is supported by herself, with her teachings held safely in her soul. Connected to the universe by a cord, she hears the lessons we have all been given. She sees the gifts that are received with the heart and knows they will be there for all eternity. But to be fully present to the beauty of itself and the world, the heart must be open.'"

go unseen and unexpressed for the rest of your life. A regular practice of visual journaling not only enables you to tap into your own wellspring of inner knowledge, creativity and inspiration, it also helps you to stay emotionally stable, physically healthy and spiritually fulfilled.

WEEK SIX

Visual Journaling as a Lifelong Practice

To encourage you to stay with the weekly schedule that you have established while working with this book, we have set up this chapter (the sixth and final week of the program) to include information, exercises, suggestions and ideas that will help you expand your visual-journaling experience into a lifelong practice.

You begin this week by learning how to strengthen the connection you have already made to your soul with an exercise that will help you discover your soul's purpose. Knowing your soul's purpose enables you to better understand its messages and the directives you will receive when life brings you face to face with important decisions and opportunities, as well as painful experiences that seem senseless until they are seen through the eyes of the soul. This exercise is followed by a fanciful visualization that takes you deep into your heart, the keeper of the soul. Using your inner eye, you will be guided to envision the landscape of your heart, which will help you see what you are holding there emotionally and spiritually.

Next, we describe a phenomenon that occurs when people do any kind of artwork or visual journaling on a continuing basis: they begin to develop recognizable, repetitive images and marks. There are examples to show you what these marks can look like, and we encourage you to review your journal work to discover your own repetitive patterns.

The final section tells you how to start your own visual-journaling support group. We also outline some of the all-important do's and don'ts that are essential when organizing any kind of group in which there will be an open exchange of personal and often very private information and emotional disclosure.

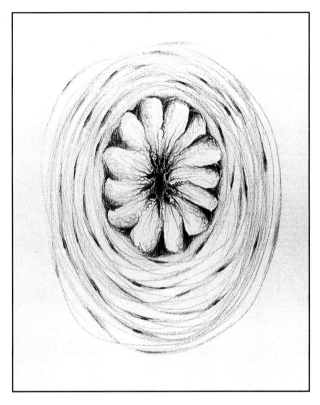

Figure 9-3. **Connected to My Soul,** *from the journal of Sabra*

"When I feel connected to my essence, to my soul, I feel safe. I do not feel the need to grasp out into the world. All I need to do is center myself, focus within, and then I will know when to reach out, when to stay within. It's a growing process, not a grasping process."

STRENGTHENING THE CONNECTION TO YOUR SOUL

It is important to know what keeps us connected to our soul, because without that connection we lose our sense of who we really are. What disconnects us from our soul is our attachment to other people's judgments and opinions. When we fear negative feedback from others, we are tempted to reshape ourselves to conform to their expectations. As children, most of us are taught to believe that what our friends and neighbors think about us is more important than what we think about ourselves. If we had to isolate the single learned belief that has caused the most damage to the soul, that would be the one.

Living our lives to please others is the fastest way to destroy the essence of who we are at the core of our being—our soul self. Fortunately, more and more people are finally coming to understand that what others think of them is irrelevant. The only opinion we ever need to be concerned about is our own. If we are not happy with

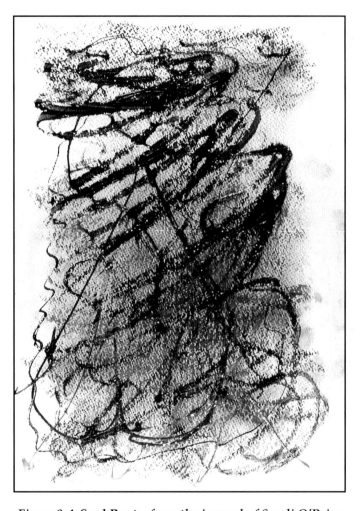

Figure 9-4. **Soul Roots,** *from the journal of Sandi O'Brien*

"This work has been life altering. My first experience with visual journaling began three years ago. Just a few minutes into the first drawing I ever did, I started to sob uncontrollably, because I realized that it was almost impossible for me to play. Today, I cherish the hours I am engaged with my journal because for me it is pure play.

"I created this drawing at a time when I was feeling very unsettled about an issue that had surfaced between me and a friend. Not knowing exactly what to do about it, I turned to my journal to ask my soul for guidance. As I began, the image that revealed itself resembled a tree with very secure roots. I then added blue to the tree, which told me that I needed to speak my truth. Then I added green, and realized I needed to speak that truth with an open heart. The message from my soul was clear: it was more important for me to maintain this relationship than to sacrifice it over this issue. I was looking for clarity from my soul and I received it."

ourselves, if we do not accept who we are, if we do not love ourselves, then all the accolades in the world will not matter. And conversely, if others hate us, reject us or disapprove of us, yet we still love and accept ourselves, then nothing they say or do will ever touch us. When we put aside attachment to other people's opinions, we open the door to the soul and forge a connection that is more powerful than any other in our lives.

As many of you may have discovered, visual journaling is one of the best ways to strengthen your connection to your soul. It allows your soul's voice to come through loud and clear. Opening that channel of communication not only enables you to receive the wisdom of its guidance, it also begins to awaken you to the notion that your existence on this planet is not a random accident and that there is more to life than just living each day to get by. That realization completes the connection between body, mind and spirit.

KNOWING YOUR SOUL PURPOSE

Most of the people who attend our visual-journaling workshops readily admit that they were motivated to join because they had been feeling an overwhelming sense of emptiness in their lives. We have found that people feel empty not because they don't have enough in their lives, but because their lives lack a sense of inner purpose—what we call soul purpose. We believe there is a reason why every person is born, that each of us is meant to accomplish something unique.

An individual's soul purpose does not

always have to be some outstanding achievement, like becoming the first female president of the United States or winning the Nobel Peace Prize. Anything that any one of us does that positively and lovingly touches even one other life is a great humanitarian accomplishment. Imagine if each person alive could positively influence and inspire just one other person. The entire population of the world would be forever changed. The fact is, we do affect others every day whether we are aware of it or not. Unfortunately, if we feel empty and purposeless, the affect may be less than loving and positive. When an individual brings a sense of purpose to even the smallest task, the results can be astounding.

Knowing your soul purpose not only strengthens your connection to your soul, it also makes it easier to trust your soul's guidance. Now you see the direction your life is meant to take as new issues and conflicts, questions and choices unfold.

EXERCISE #1

Discovering Your Soul Purpose

There are always people who just seem to know what their soul purpose is, and they follow it with uninterrupted dedication. But most of us need a little help. So that you can understand your soul's guidance as you continue to face conflicting issues and difficult choices, this exercise guides you into your heart center where you can more readily connect with the voice of your soul. From there, you ask your soul for a symbol that represents your purpose in this lifetime.

When you are ready, turn once again to the next two side-by-side blank pages in your journal and write down your intention. It should in some way reflect your desire to access a symbol that represents your soul purpose. Then get into a comfortable position and follow the directions in the next guided visualization. As always, feel free to use movement or sound.

- Close your eyes and take several deep breaths. Allow yourself to become fully present to your physical body by paying close attention to the rise and fall of your chest as you breathe in and out. Continue doing this until you feel completely connected to your body.
- Imagine that your conscious awareness is a tiny bead of light nestled deep within your mind, and that you are able to move that tiny bead anywhere in your body that you like.
- Focus your attention on your heart center. Imagine that this tiny bead of light, the light of your conscious awareness, is drifting gently down toward your heart center. Sense its presence deep within your heart.
- With your conscious awareness now present within your heart, imagine opening the channel of communication with your soul. Ask your soul to present you with a symbol that represents its purpose for you in this lifetime.
- When you know what that symbol is, open your eyes and draw it in your journal.

Self-Exploration Questions

After you complete your drawing, look at this symbol for a while. Then, when you are ready, use the next free page of your journal to write your responses to the self-exploration questions that follow. Your responses will help you clarify the meaning of this symbol.

1. What do you feel your soul-purpose symbol means?
2. If this symbol could speak, what would it say to you?
3. What does it tell you about your life's purpose?
4. Do the colors you used have any special meaning?
5. Has this symbol ever come up for you before? If so, in what context?
6. Describe what you now feel is your life's purpose.
7. How does it fit in with your life right now?
8. How do you see your soul purpose manifesting in your life in the future?
9. If you were to follow the direction of your soul purpose, what changes would you need to make in your life?
10. Do you have any fears or trepidations about following this direction? If so, what are they?
11. If you feel apprehensive about your soul purpose, what might this feeling be trying to teach you?
12. Has the idea of this particular soul purpose, as indicated by the symbol, ever presented itself to you in your life or consciousness before? If so, in what way?
13. What can you start doing today to begin living out your soul's purpose?

EXAMPLES OF SOUL-PURPOSE SYMBOLS

If you are having difficulty understanding what your soul-purpose symbol means even after answering the self-exploration questions, then perhaps the next four examples of soul-purpose symbol drawings might help. Also included are quotes from each journaler that describe what they felt their symbol meant. We hope these examples will help you see your own symbol from a different perspective that might shed some light on its meaning.

As we pointed out before, your soul purpose may not be a specific career-related goal or a definable accomplishment. It may be something more like the directive that Cherie received from her soul-purpose symbol (Figure 9-5). The message she got was to let her life flow; that her purpose was to overflow. Similarly, your symbol might tell you, for example, to trust in your own power to make decisions and create changes in your life. Or your symbol might say that if you nurture your sense of inner peace, you can become an inspiring source of peace and joy to others. (This is not to rule out that your symbol might, in fact, be telling you to pursue a specific goal).

The important thing is to keep an open mind and heart and not allow yourself to be disappointed if your symbol is not what you expected. Remember, spirit works in unpredictable ways. What you regard as a disappointing message may be the most exciting direction your life could take.

If you still are not clear on the meaning of your soul-purpose symbol, then you may need to just live with it for a while. The best way to do that is to remove the page from your journal and

Figure 9-5. **Expansive Soul,** *from the journal of Cherie*

"This image of my soul's purpose is so expansive and fluid that it feels like it surrounds, accommodates and feeds me. It bubbles up out of the depths, surrounding me with nurturing, and caring for me on this journey. It holds my hand sometimes and then embraces me. It is a full body, mind and heart experience of love and joy.

"As I drew this soul expression, it felt too expansive to capture on paper, and it feels so absolutely personal. It reminds me that I am not alone—this is one of the big messages I hear from it over and over. If only I can keep from being fearful, my connection will always be strong. My soul keeps reminding me, 'I am with you.' It tells me to be in flow; my purpose is to overflow."

142

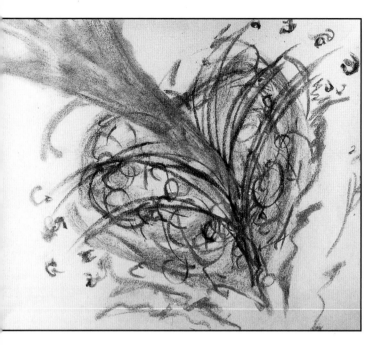

Figure 9-6. **The Soul of Movement,** *from the journal of Christina*

"As this symbol speaks, I hear it say that I am expansive, wider than I can imagine. I am full of space and breath, changing and infinite. See what is possible if you open yourself? We can move, we can breathe, we can transform. Through the eyes of the soul, all of us are accepted and welcomed just as we are. My life's purpose, as it is communicated through my soul, is for me to accept myself."

Figure 9-7. **The Goddess Brings Gifts,** *from the journal of Ishmira Kathleen Thoma*

"I don't know who I really am, but I can feel it. Words cannot go there. Dancing goes there. Color goes there. Light, drumming, chanting go there. When I can see light, energy and love, fear disappears. I am told by this symbol that my purpose is to bring the goddess energies through my work, and I know that this is the feminine energy of nurturing and light."

Figure 9-8. **Letting My Soul Shine,** *from the journal of Birgitta Grimm*

"I have always been the one who was expected to be the core of my family—to be the teacher. But I have never wanted to be that person. It felt like a burden to my soul. This symbol tells me that my soul wants to shine. It also tells me that I do not need to hold other souls under my spell. If I let my soul shine by following its guidance and releasing the burden, then other souls can fly on their own power."

tape it to a wall where you can see it every day. After some time passes, you may discover that suddenly your symbol makes sense.

REMAINING CONGRUENT WITH YOUR SOUL PURPOSE

The more you do visual journaling, the more you can trust that part of yourself that wants to remain congruent with your soul purpose. As you grow in your ability to trust yourself and your soul's guidance, you will learn how to feel comfortable taking appropriate risks; you will feel safe in an often unsafe world. Inner trust and security combined with the ultimate understanding of soul purpose enable a previously frightened person to say no to an abusive spouse, move away from a controlling parent, or reject any situation that threatens his or her well-being.

EXERCISE #2

Drawing the Landscape of Your Heart

If there is one place in the body where the soul might dwell, we feel that it is most likely the heart. After all, the heart is the organ most responsive to our feelings and emotions. For centuries, writers and poets have referred to the heart as the place from which love grows, sadness pines and joy overflows. Love, longing, grief, sadness, desire and joy—these are the province of heart and soul, not the mind.

In this exercise, you are guided to imagine what your heart would look like if it were a landscape. Would it be rocky and barren or lush and green? Would it be day or night? Would the sky be clear and bright or filled with clouds? Who or what might be living in this landscape? What is their purpose there? Is your heart's landscape welcoming and open or forbidding and closed? How you see your heart will tell you who you are, what you love, how you express that love, what gives you joy, what makes you sad, and what you desire. When you combine these elements with what you know about your soul purpose, you will have all you need to live the life you were brought into this world to experience.

When you are ready to begin, turn to the next two side-by-side blank pages in your journal and write down your intention. It should reflect your desire to envision the landscape of your heart. Then get into a comfortable position and follow the directions. Use movement or sound if you like.

- Close your eyes and take three long, slow, deep breaths. Concentrate your attention on the rise and fall of your chest. Feel the air move in and out of your lungs. Now take three more deep breaths, and imagine breathing in light and breathing out color— any color at all. Take three more breaths, and again breathe in light and breathe out color. Feel your body relax more with each exhalation. Continue breathing in light and exhaling color until you feel completely relaxed and comfortable.
- Now breathe normally and allow your attention to move away from your breathing and drift toward your heart center.
- Hold your focus on your heart center and allow yourself to become present there. When you are able to connect with the feelings inside your heart, imagine what those feelings would look like if they were a landscape.
- What kind of terrain does this landscape have? What kind of vegetation grows there? What color is the sky? Are there clouds? Is it stormy or calm? Day or night? Are there trees or flowers or roads or buildings in your heart's landscape? Are there living entities there? What are they and what is their purpose?
- When you sense what your heart's landscape would look like, open your eyes and draw it.

When you have completed your drawing, prop or tape it up someplace where you can look at it from a distance. Now sit down and take a good, long look at it. When you are ready, answer the self-exploration questions.

Self-Exploration Questions

This drawing represents metaphorically what you hold emotionally and spiritually inside your heart. First, read through the questions, and when you are ready to answer them, use the next free page in your journal. Your responses will help you understand what your heart feels, what it desires and even what it may need.

1. As you look at this drawing of your heart's landscape, how does it make you feel?
2. Does anything about it surprise you? If so, what?
3. What does this landscape tell you about your heart?
4. How do the colors make you feel?
5. Is there anything that disturbs you? If so, describe what and why.
6. Write a few sentences that explain what you like best about your drawing.
7. What have you learned from it about your heart?

USING LARGER FORMATS AND DIFFERENT MEDIA

Journal drawing often sparks the desire to create larger pieces and to work in different media. Although we have included several of these larger pieces and a few of the works in different media throughout the book, we want to explain a little bit about the varied media and

Figure 9-9. **The Landscape of My Heart,** *from the journal of Kate Siekierski*

"This landscape of my heart tells me that my heart and I are connected to the universe. The power and flow of being alive move from the universe through me and into my heart. The sun warms my heart, the night sky connects me, the beautiful purple majestic mountains support me. In the bottom of the landscape is the tension that gets in the way of my feeling alive. It is being sent into the earth, because I don't need it. The llama is in my heart to help me release the tension."

materials some of our journalers use, with the hope that you might be inspired to expand your journal work in new directions.

Many of our journalers first began their ventures into larger formats by working on bigger pieces of drawing paper. When that was not enough, they moved on to cardboard, stretched canvas, Masonite board and even sheets of plywood. Others wanted to work with three-dimensional materials, so they began to experiment with clay, both the self-hardening kind and the more traditional kiln-fired varieties. Some journalers began to work with wood, carving or constructing sculptures, boxes or environments and making hanging mobiles. A few adventurous souls even tried working in metal.

But for some of our journalers, bigger was not necessarily better. These people were perfectly happy with the boundaries of their journals, but they wanted to use different kinds of materials. One journaler glued Astroturf to her drawings for added texture. Another began gluing sandpaper to her journal pages and rubbing paint and pastels into it. Yet another journaler found heaven in her compost pile as dried corn husks, leaves and shriveled grass became the adjunct materials of choice to accompany her water colors and pastels. Glitter, sand paint, colored glue and Day-Glo paint did the trick for other journalers who wanted to give their drawings a bit of oomph.

Our point here is to let you know that anything goes when it comes to expressing your deepest angst, your inner conflicts or your heart's greatest desires. If you find yourself in the midst of a creative urge to try something different, do

Figure 9-10. **Oh, My Goodness!,** *from the journal of Robin Boyd*

"My intention is to travel the terrain of my heart without criticism or judgment and to know what is in my heart.

"Oh, my goodness. I had no idea my heart was so beautiful. I am in love with the world, the explosive busyness of it all. I am in love with my connection. I am in love with being in love with the world—so vibrant and dark, intense and bright and busy! The colors make me feel alone, yet so much a part of everything. So full of vision, possibility, excitement! Only the birds have like companions. The snake, the caribou and the human are all alone among their kind. But we are all a part of the greater whole, so we are not alone.

"I am much richer than I ever thought. I like the way my heart is anchored, yet I am still able to journey far. I can always return to the source. I know this. I take in sustenance. I take in knowledge. Then I travel to the light and back again."

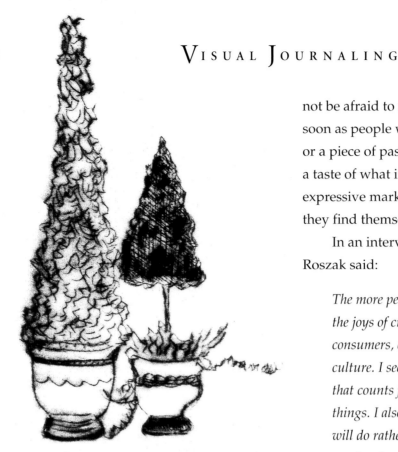

Figure 9-11. **Topiary Trees,** *a metal etching by* **Carole Patterson**

"Since first taking pastel in hand, a new and exciting world has opened to me. My journey began with a chance meeting with a friend who excitedly told me about a visual-journaling group she attended, and encouraged me to join. Looking for something more than the treadmill I was on, and with the reassurance that no art experience was required, I jumped at the invitation. I wouldn't become aware until later how much that encounter would change my life.

"The safe and accepting atmosphere of the group enabled me to discover a part of myself that I had always hoped was there but was never able to discover. Refocusing the creation of art from my head to my heart and recalling the childhood freedom to express myself helped awaken a strong urge to create. A year later, I took a leave of absence from work and started art classes. I am excited with my life and the creative work that is now a main focus."

not be afraid to follow it. We have found that as soon as people who have never had a paint brush or a piece of pastel chalk in their hands before get a taste of what it feels like to make colorful, expressive marks on paper, it is not long before they find themselves craving more.

In an interview, ecopsychologist Theodore Roszak said:

> *The more people have time to experience the joys of creativity, the less they will be consumers, especially of mass-produced culture. I see that as a kind of new wealth that counts for more than owning material things. I also see art as something people will do rather than consume, and do it as a natural part of their lives; creative endeavors are a form of profound spiritual satisfaction.*

We agree, and the more we can turn people on to the fun and emotional gratification that come from visual journaling, the less we will all need to depend on material fast fixes as the only way to satisfy our inner longings.

IMAGISTIC SIGNATURES AND PERSONAL POWER STROKES

When people do visual journaling or any kind of artwork on a regular basis, they develop repetitive marks or images, which we call *imagistic signatures* and *personal power strokes.* Most people are unaware that they repeat certain lines, shapes, forms or images. Once they do become aware and make an effort to identify their specific repetitive marks and images, they begin

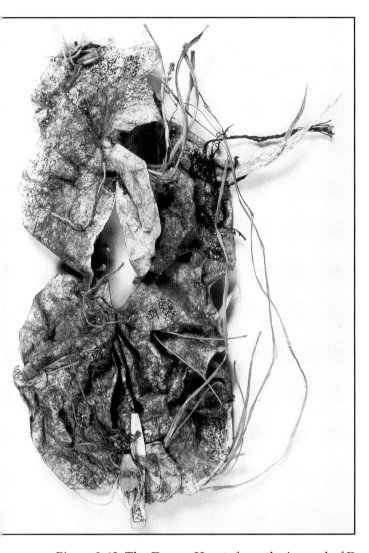

to understand the subconscious meanings of these marks.

In this section, we explain what repetitive marks and images are so that you can identify your own repetitive imagistic patterns. As you learn to identify them, you will also see how they convey important information about who you are and who you are becoming. They are, in essence, a form of imagistic shorthand that can be used, as you continue doing your journal work, to reinforce the transformation that is taking place within you.

An imagistic signature is a particular type of line, shape or form that an individual develops over time. It is in some way characteristic of that person, and it develops in much the same way as a written signature. It also, like a written signature, becomes so uniquely individual that it can be used as a means of personal identification.

Some examples of repetitive lines, shapes and forms that comprise imagistic signatures are

Figure 9-12. **The Donna Heart,** *from the journal of Donna DiGiuseppe*

"This is my heart's landscape. It seemed appropriate to use herbs, corn husks, a tree root, crystals, beads, and glitter on paper covered with pastels. I even glued on the tissue I used to smudge my pastels onto the paper. It makes me feel very alive, organic, balanced, multidimensional and creative. It tapped my inner reservoir.

"This piece tells me that my heart is growing, thirsty to thrive. It wants to be touched and seen. It reaches out, but it also has crevices for places to hide. It is a place of rest and also surprise. It is a happy, young heart with a twist of old. The green of the herbs and grasses makes me feel soft and feminine; the brown leaves make me feel earthy and grounded. I like that I can hang it up and look at it. It falls forward, and this feels like an outpouring or outflow of my heart into space. It makes me feel like I have a presence, like I am connected organically to my environment and the space I live in.

"I have learned that my heart lives and dies. That it opens and closes. It speaks to me and I listen. My heart has all feelings. It is my reservoir of emotion. I love my heart. I have a good and happy, creative heart. My heart shows me and teaches me about myself. My heart can share."

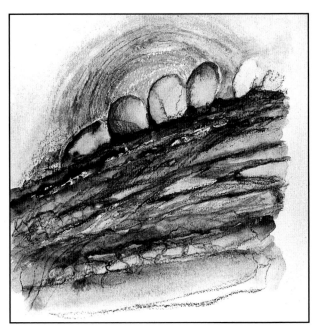

Figure 9-13. From the journal of Adele Karbowski

Figure 9-14. From the journal of Adele Karbowski

spirals, squares, triangles, circles and various kinds of geometric or abstract shapes. These lines, shapes and forms usually evolve into more complex images such as crosses, flowers, suns, mountain shapes, lightning bolts, tree forms, water, birds and snakes. These signature images often find their way into most of the drawings a journaler produces.

A personal power stroke is a line or mark that is repeated again and again in different drawings. The repetitive line or mark is usually made with quick and often unconscious hand movements. Like an imagistic signature, a personal power stroke is also highly characteristic of the individual.

The journal drawing that is used as the cover piece in this book was done by one of our journalers, Adele Karbowski. That drawing, along with two others by Adele (Figures 9-13 and 9-14) are

classic examples of how an imagistic signature constantly reappears in different drawings. For Adele, egg shapes or podlike forms became her imagistic signature. As they developed, they started to appear in about eighty percent of her work. When Adele talks about these shapes, she refers to them as the containers for her new beliefs, actions and behaviors. These containers or pods, she tells us, are in the process of giving birth to her new self.

Power strokes do not usually form a completed image the way an imagistic signature often does. Power strokes are more like gestures that make up a larger form or shape. They tend to be the building blocks or structural elements of a specific symbol or image. Some examples of power strokes are crossed lines, parallel lines, triangles, circles, dots and dashes, wavy lines and slanted and slash lines. The triangular shapes in

Figures 9-15, 9-16 and 9-17 are the personal power strokes that Cherie uses frequently to form mountains, teeth and sometimes just abstract pattern designs.

We began calling these repetitive marks "personal power strokes" because our journalers told us that using them made them feel more powerful. As one journaler put it, "When I'm using my power stroke, I feel as though I am revealing a deep inner truth about myself. I also feel more balanced and energized inside, like I am reconnecting to a symbolic inner guidance system."

At the end of each six-week program, we ask our workshop participants to go back through all the journal work they have produced, which can be anywhere from twelve to thirty pieces of artwork, and identify their own imagistic signatures and personal power strokes. We would like to suggest that you also take the time to do this. If you do, you will begin to see your own repetitive imagistic patterns and how they express some inner truth or positive aspect of yourself that is helping you evolve to your fullest potential.

The Benefits of Working with a Group

Unless you start your own visual-journaling group, there is one advantage that our workshop participants have that you do not have working alone—they get to share their work with each other. Being part of a visual-journaling group is

Figures 9-15, 9-16, and 9-17. From the journal of Cherie

152

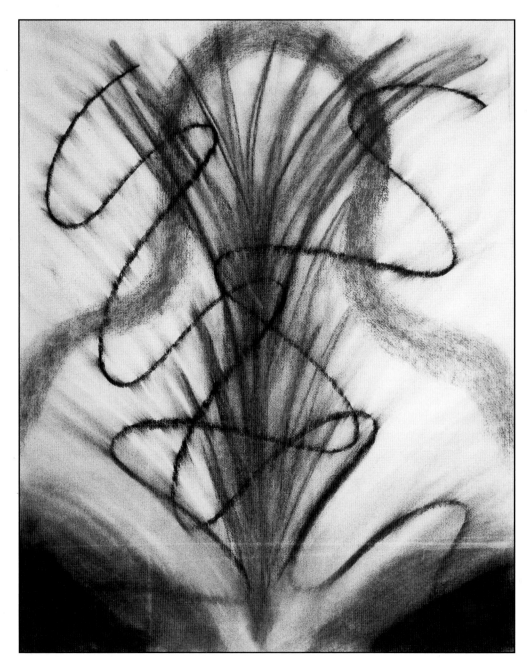

Figure 9-18. **Search for Soul,** *from the journal of Lisa Slattery*

"My soul winds its way through life searching for itself. It finds its true colors and shapes, yet cannot be contained. When I connect with my infinity, I know I am home."

very powerful, because something transformative and healing takes place when group members show each other their artwork and reveal what they have learned about themselves. Something healing and transforming also happens as we listen to other people express their feelings and share their experiences: we begin to understand that we are not alone. We see that everyone feels pain and confusion from time to time, and that others have also suffered losses similar to our own. There is comfort in the sharing of our humanness.

STARTING YOUR OWN VISUAL-JOURNALING GROUP

If you would like to organize your own visual-journaling group, the information that follows will help you get started. It includes operating guidelines and some of the more important do's and don'ts that go into running any kind of group in which there will be an open exchange of personal and often very private information.

• **There are two ways to form a group.**

1. Call several people you know who you think might be interested in visual journaling and invite them to join.

   Keep the group small. More than six or eight people make it difficult for each person to have time to share.

2. Make up a flyer or announcement and post it at local bookstores, health-food stores and anywhere else where the kind of people who might be attracted to such a group would see it.

• **This is a support group, not a therapy group.**

Unless you are a trained counselor, psychotherapist or expressive-art therapist, it is extremely important to clearly communicate to each and every person who joins that this is a support group, not a therapy group. Ask each person to check their own intention to be sure that they are not expecting this support group to be a substitute for group therapy.

• **Set up your group to meet on a regular basis.**

We have found that meeting once a week for two hours enables journalers to maintain a feeling of consistency in their journaling practice. It is also advisable to decide on a specific number of weeks during which the group will meet and stick with that schedule.

• **Begin with the six-week program.**

It is best to begin your group by following the six-week program in this book. If group members want to go beyond the initial six weeks, everyone should have a voice in deciding on the number of weeks to continue.

• **Set up procedural guidelines and ask everyone to follow them.**

The guidelines we recommend are the same as those we use with our groups.

1. One person should be designated as group moderator. That can be the person who organizes the group, or someone chosen by vote.

2. It is the moderator's job to start and end the sessions on time and keep the group moving so that each person has time to speak and share their work and experiences.

3. Ask each person to respect every group member's right to privacy by observing the following rule of confidentiality: No one may mention any other group member's name outside the group, and each person must agree that anything said in group will not be repeated outside the group.

4. The primary function of any support group is to provide an environment in which each member feels safe to express deep feelings

without fear of judgment or criticism. Therefore, everyone must agree to suspend all judgment when entering the group.

5. Never try to interpret another group member's artwork. You can discuss and comment on the process without interpreting the work itself by using "I" statements, such as, "When I look at your images, I see . . ." This way, you can share your insights while honoring the other person's interpretation.

6. Each member is asked to listen attentively, compassionately and nonjudgmentally as other members share their work, thoughts and feelings.

7. One group member should never be allowed to dominate the group. Sharing one's visual-journaling experiences and the corresponding emotions that can surface while doing this work can be very powerful for both the group and the individual. However, if one member begins to monopolize the group's time and tries to focus on dealing with intense emotions that are inappropriate for a nontherapy support group, or wants the group to help solve a particular problem, the moderator should remind that individual that it is time to move on so that everyone can participate.

8. Limit the amount of time each person has to talk about their work. Ten minutes per person is about all a group can tolerate before they begin to get fidgety.

9. Emphasize starting on time, since waiting for latecomers is annoying and discourages punctuality.

10. End your meetings on time. Running over

can get quickly out of hand and makes it difficult to reinforce the guideline that one person should not monopolize the time.

11. Suggest that each group member have a therapist or counselor that he or she can call on if emotions or feelings surface that require additional support.

BEYOND THE SIX-WEEK PROGRAM

To continue your visual-journaling work beyond this six-week program, the following suggestions should help keep you going:

1. Do a check-in drawing every day or every other day to establish what you are feeling, experiencing or in need of expressing emotionally, physically or spiritually. This enables you to determine if certain feelings or emotions need further exploration.

2. If your check-in drawing reveals that you are conflicted, confused, or emotionally or creatively blocked, then focus on the issue creating the problem. Move your awareness into your heart center and ask your soul to present you with a symbol or image that best expresses what you need to know, learn or do.

3. If you are struggling with the need to make a decision—let's say whether or not to take a new job or stay in a relationship—close your eyes and imagine yourself in each situation: working at the new job versus remaining where you are; staying in the relationship versus leaving it. Then imagine how each option would feel. When you know, draw images that best express the feeling of each

option. You will know as soon as you look at your drawings which situation your soul wants you to pursue.

Although this concludes your six-week visual-journaling program, we hope your desire to continue using visual journaling to give voice to your soul does not end here. As our other journalers have told us, once you learn how to listen to your soul, you will never be content to live without it. To know that at all times you carry within the divine wisdom to guide you through life's darkest moments is the greatest gift of all.

BIBLIOGRAPHY

Anderson, Mary. *Color Therapy*. New ed. Wellingborough, England: Aquarian Press, 1990.

Arrien, Angeles. *Signs of Life: The Five Universal Shapes and How to Use Them*. Sonoma, CA: Arcus Publishing, 1992.

Babbitt, Edwin S. *Principles of Light and Color: The Healing Power of Color*. Secaucus, NJ: Citadel Press, 1967.

Birren, Farber. *The Symbolism of Color*. Secaucus, NJ: Citadel Press, 1988.

Cameron, Julia. *The Artist's Way: A Spiritual Path to Higher Creativity*, Los Angeles: Jeremy P. Tarcher, 1992.

————. *The Vein of Gold: A Journey to Your Creative Heart*. New York: Jeremy P. Tarcher/Putnam Books, 1996.

Capacchione, Lucia. *The Picture of Health: Healing Your Life with Art*. Santa Monica, CA: Hay House, 1990.

————. *The Creative Journal: The Art of Finding Yourself*. North Hollywood, CA: Newcastle Publishing, 1989.

Cooper, J. C. *An Illustrated Encyclopedia of Traditional Symbols*. London: Thames & Hudson, 1988.

Cornell, Judith. *Drawing the Light from Within*. Wheaton, IL: Quest Books, 1997.

————. *Mandala: Luminous Symbols for Healing*. Wheaton, IL: Quest Books, 1994.

Fezler, William. *Imagery for Healing, Knowledge, and Power*. New York: Simon and Schuster, 1990.

Fontana, David. *The Secret Language of Symbols: A Visual Key to Symbols and Their Meanings*. San Francisco: Chronicle Books, 1993.

Fox, Matthew. *A Spirituality Named Compassion*. New York: HarperCollins Publishers, 1990.

Furth, Gregg M. *The Secret World of Drawings*. Boston: Sigo Press, 1988.

Gallegos, Eligio Stephen. *Animals of the Four Winds: Integrating Thinking, Sensing, Feeling and Imagery*. Santa Fe: Moon Bear Press, 1991.

Gawain, Shakti. *Creative Visualization*. New York: Bantam New Age, 1979.

Gombel, Theo. *Healing Through Colour*. Saffron Walden, England: C. W. Daniel Company, 1980.

Harman, Willis, and Howard Rheingold. *Higher Creativity: Liberating the Unconscious for Breakthrough Insights*. Los Angeles: Jeremy P. Tarcher, 1984.

Hillman, James. *The Soul's Code: In Search of Character and Calling*. New York: Random House, 1996.

Kryder, Rowena Pattee. *Sacred Ground to Sacred Earth*. Santa Fe: Bear & Co. Publishing, 1994.

London, Peter. *No More Second-Hand Art: Awakening the Artist Within*. Boston: Shambala Publications, 1989.

Lusser Rico, Gabriele. *Writing the Natural Way*. Los Angeles: Jeremy P. Tarcher, 1983.

Markova, Dawna. *No Enemies Within: A Creative Process for Discovering What's Right About What's Wrong*. Berkeley: Conari Press, 1994.

Markowitz, Gary, and Anajelae Rhoads, eds. *One Source Sacred Journey: A Celebration of Spirit and Art*. Paia, HI: Markowitz Publishing, 1997.

McNiff, Shaun. *Art as Medicine*. Boston: Shambhala Publications, 1992.

Moore, Thomas. *Care of the Soul: A Guide for Cultivating Depth and Sacredness in Everyday Life*. New York: HarperCollins Publishers, 1992.

Myss, C. *Why People Don't Heal and How They Can*. New York: Harmony Books, 1997.

Nelson, Mary Carroll. *Artists of the Spirit: New Prophets in Art and Mysticism*. Sonoma, CA: Arcus Publishing, 1994.

Oldfield, Harry, and Roger Coghill. *The Dark Side of the Brain*. Rockport, MA: Element Books, 1988.

Phillips, Jan. *Marry Your Muse: Making a Lasting Commitment to Your Creativity*. Wheaton, IL: Quest Books, 1997.

Rhyne, Janie. *The Gestalt Art Experience: Creative Process and Expressive Therapy*. Chicago: Magnolia Street Publishers, 1984.

Rogers, Natalie. *The Creative Connection: Expressive Arts as Healing*. Palo Alto, CA: Science & Behavior Books, 1993.

Samuels, Michael. *Seeing with the Mind's Eye*. New York: Random House, 1993.

Samuels, Michael, and M. Rockwood Lane. *Creative Healing: How to Heal Yourself by Tapping Your Hidden Creativity*. New York: HarperCollins/HarperSanFrancisco, 1998.

Shealy, Norman C. *Miracles Do Happen*. Rockport, MA: Element Books, 1995.

Siegel, Bernie. *Peace, Love and Healing: The Bodymind and the Path to Self-Healing and Exploration*. New York: Harper & Row, 1989.

Sperry, Roger. *Science and Moral Priority: Merging Mind, Brain, and Human Values*. New York: Columbia University Press, 1983.

Walters, J. Donald. *Art as a Hidden Message: A Guide to Self-Realization*. Nevada City, CA: Crystal Clarity, 1997.

ABOUT THE AUTHORS

BARBARA GANIM, M.A.E., C.H.C., is director of the Institute for the Expressive Arts at Salve Regina University in Newport, Rhode Island, where she also teaches expressive art therapy in the Holistic Counseling Graduate Program. She is an expressive art therapist and a certified holistic counselor whose work in private practice focuses primarily on the use of art, imagery and visualization to help people who are suffering from life-threatening illnesses. For the past eight years, Barbara has been a member of the clinical staff at the Hope Center for Cancer Support, also in Providence, where she facilitates art-and-healing cancer support groups. She has worked as an expressive art therapist at Talbot Center: Women's Drug and Alcohol Day-Treatment Program in Providence, Rhode Island. Barbara is the author of *Art and Healing: Using Expressive Art to Heal Your Body, Mind, and Spirit* (Random House/Three Rivers Press, 1999). She lives in North Kingstown, Rhode Island.

SUSAN FOX, M.A.E., C.H.C., is a certified holistic counselor, an expressive art therapist and cofounder of The Center for Holistic Development in Wickford, Rhode Island. Her private practice is primarily focused on the use of art for emotional, physical and spiritual healing. She is currently on the faculty of the Institute for the Expressive Arts at Salve Regina University in Newport, Rhode Island, where she teaches expressive art therapy in the Holistic Counseling Graduate Program. In addition to teaching and her private practice, Susan has been a member of the clinical staff at the Hope Center for Cancer Support in Providence, where, for the last eight years, she has facilitated art-and-healing cancer support groups. She was also an expressive art therapist at Highpoint Drug and Alcohol Treatment Center in North Kingstown, and Edgehill Newport, a residential drug-and-alcohol treatment program in Newport.

If you would like to reach the authors or be put on a current mailing list for a schedule of upcoming lectures and workshops, contact Barbara Ganim or Susan Fox at the following address:

Art as the Spirit of Healing
PO Box 1176
North Kingstown, RI 02852

The authors may also be available for workshops and presentations at conferences and special events.

◆ ◆ ◆

If you are interested in learning how to use expressive art for healing in psychotherapy, medical caregiving and education, call or write Salve Regina University, Newport, Rhode Island, for further information on the programs listed below:

Salve Regina University
100 Ochre Point Avenue
Newport, RI 02840-4192
800-321-7124 or 401-847-6650, ext. 2157

GRADUATE PROGRAM IN HOLISTIC COUNSELING

A sixty-credit M.A. degree in Holistic Counseling with a C.A.G.S. (Certificate in Advanced Graduate Study) in the Expressive Arts

GRADUATE CREDIT CERTIFICATE PROGRAM IN THE EXPRESSIVE ARTS

A program for individuals with a master's degree in psychotherapy or a related field

THE INSTITUTE FOR THE EXPRESSIVE ARTS

Professional Development Certificate Program in Healing with the Expressive Arts for Medical Caregivers, Counselors and Educators, a non-credit, two-week intensive training

161

QUEST BOOKS
are published by
The Theosophical Society in America,
Wheaton, Illinois 60189-0270,
a branch of a world fellowship,
a membership organization
dedicated to the promotion of the unity of
humanity and the encouragement of the study of
religion, philosophy, and science, to the end that
we may better understand ourselves and our place in
the universe. The Society stands for complete
freedom of individual search and belief.
For further information about its activities,
write, call 1-800-669-1571, e-mail olcott@theosophia.org,
or consult its Web page: http://www.theosophical.org

The Theosophical Publishing House
is aided by the generous support of
THE KERN FOUNDATION,
a trust established by Herbert A. Kern
and dedicated to Theosophical education.